W9-AXM-382

Hiking Virginia's National Forests

"A good guide to carry in your pocket or pack . . . will get you through the tough spots."
—*Richmond* (VA) *Times-Dispatch*

"Describes more than 50 trails in the George Washington and Jefferson national forests, giving distances, elevations, difficulty and tips on bush-whacking and wilderness camping."
—*Mid-Atlantic Country*

"For hikers who . . . want to find, plan, and enjoy interesting walks according to their abilities and inclinations . . . extremely useful . . . strongly recommended."
—*Appalachia*

Hiking Virginia's National Forests

Fifth Edition

by

Karin Wuertz-Schaefer

An East Woods Book

The Globe Pequot Press

Old Saybrook, Connecticut

Maps generated from original art work by Robert J. Schaefer

Library of Congress Cataloging-in-Publication Data

Wuertz-Schaefer, Karin.
    Hiking Virginia's national forests / by Karin Wuertz-Schaefer. — 5th ed.
        p.   cm.
    An East Woods book.
    Includes bibliographical references.
    ISBN 1-56440-374-2
    1. Hiking—George Washington National Forest (Va. and W. Va.)—
Guidebooks. 2. Hiking—Jefferson National Forest—Guidebooks.
3. George Washington National Forest (Va. and W. Va.)—Guidebooks.
4. Jefferson National Forest—Guidebooks.
GV199.42.G45W84 1994
796.5'1'09755—dc20   93-39829
                                                 CIP

♻ This book is printed on recycled paper.
Manufactured in the United States of America
Fifth Edition/Fifth Printing

Contents

George Washington National Forest

Jefferson National Forest

George Washington National Forest

1 Big Schloss
2 Laurel Fork
3 Ramsey's Draft
4 Crawford Mountain
5 Elliott Knob
6 Saint Mary's

Jefferson National Forest

7 James River Face
8 Mountain Lake
9 Peters Mountain
10 Mount Rogers

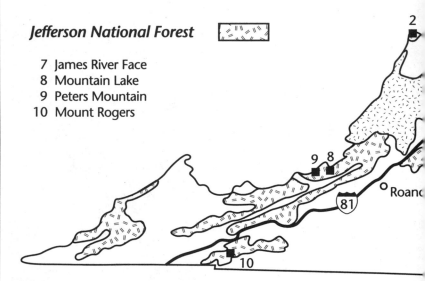

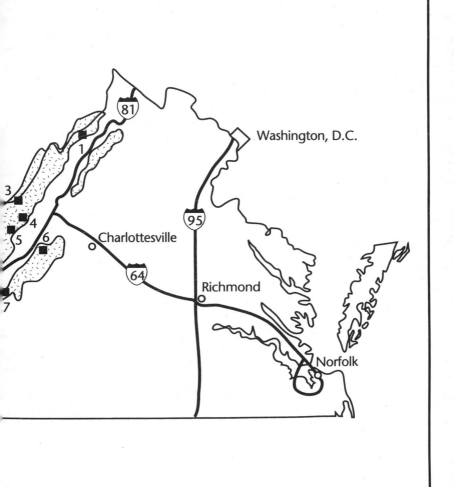

List of Maps

Photography Credits

Acknowledgments

I would like to thank the many people without whom this book would long since have gone out of print. My gratitude goes especially to all the scouts who did most of the legwork verifying the trails and recording any changes: Dean Amel, Lynn Cameron, Ernie Dickerman, Vernon Garber, Pat and Marilyn Lockhart, David Jenkins, and Gary Slemp. The staffs of the George Washington and Jefferson national forests have also been very helpful in all aspects of gathering information.

And last, but not least, I would like to thank my husband, Bob, for his support and help throughout the years of writing and revising, not to mention drawing and redrawing the maps for this book. Without him the project would have foundered long ago.

Conservation Efforts

This book is the result of the combined efforts of local members of the Sierra Club and the Virginia Wilderness Committee, who invite all who enjoy and cherish the beautiful Virginia mountains to join their efforts to protect them.

Sierra Club
730 Polk Street
San Francisco, CA 94109

Virginia Wilderness Committee
Route 1, Box 156
Swoope, VA 24479

Hiking Virginia's
National Forests

Introduction

The national forests of Virginia—George Washington National Forest in the northwest and Jefferson National Forest in the southwest—encompass large areas of mountains and forests laced with clear streams. Wildlife is abundant, and many trails crisscross the region.

Looking at road maps for most regions of the United States, you will see large patches of green, indicating national forests. This is misleading, for although national forest boundaries have been authorized by Congress, there is much privately owned land within them. The U.S. Forest Service has not been able to purchase all of the land in the authorized regions. In the past, logged-over tracts were often offered for sale to the federal government because the owners had no further use for them and did not want to invest money in reforestation programs. Now many of these regions are beginning to mature and assume appearances close to their original ones.

Trying to compile a trail guide to all of both national forests in Virginia would have been a monumental task. Instead, we have selected ten areas that are outstanding for various reasons. These tracts are largely self-contained units bounded by roads and often by private land. Human intrusion is minimal, and each area, in its own way, is unique.

We want this book to give you a taste for hiking in the forests. There are many additional places that have good trails and are worth exploring. A number of wilderness areas in Virginia have been established by Congress since this book was first published in 1977. Many recreation sites and campgrounds (generally levying a small fee) exist. But wilderness camping is often available if you hike a few miles along a trail.

Even in the places covered by this book, you may find obscure and unmaintained trails. We have tried to describe all the ones

1

that can be found and followed with reasonable care, but surprises are still possible. The Forest Service budget provides some money for trail maintenance, and their crews do most of the heavy work, such as clearing away severe obstructions or performing major relocations of the trails. Citizens' organizations, relying on volunteers, can maintain only a few trails.

The Appalachian Trail (AT) is part of the trail system in many areas covered by this guide. If you are interested in learning more about the AT—especially elsewhere in the state—we suggest you obtain the Appalachian Trail Guide to Central & Southwest Virginia, published by the Appalachian Trail Conference (P.O. Box 807, Harpers Ferry, WV 25425).

In some places you will find small cabins owned and maintained by the Potomac Appalachian Trail Club. These cabins are locked, but the general public as well as club members may make reservations for their use. Contact the club for additional information well in advance of your trip. The address: Potomac Appalachian Trail Club, 1718 N Street, N. W., Washington, DC 20036; telephone: (202) 638–5306.

Much of the George Washington and Jefferson national forests is habitat for the black bear and the bobcat, although both are extremely wary and rarely seen. On our hikes and camping trips we have seen and heard deer, bears, salamanders, skunks, opossums, and raccoons as well as beavers, squirrels, and other rodents. Bird life is varied—turkeys, ruffed grouse, ravens, pileated woodpeckers, barred and screech owls, and whip-poor-wills are just a few of the many, many species, both summer and winter residents, that we have identified. You may find additional denizens of the woods, too numerous to list. A good number of streams support trout. Please remember that the hunting and fishing laws of the state of Virginia are applicable in those portions of the national forest that lie within the state's boundaries. Some trails also cross into West Virginia, and, of course, West Virginia hunting and fishing laws apply there. We have not attempted to define political boundaries in this book. If in doubt, check with the district ranger's office.

National forests differ from national parks in several respects. The national forests are administered by the Forest Service under the U.S. Department of Agriculture, while national parks are managed by the National Park Service under the U.S. Department of the Interior. The management philosophy for these public resources is also profoundly different. National forests are managed under the multiple-use concept and are open to many kinds of human activity, including logging, road building, dams, hunting, fishing, hiking, and camping. Not so in the national parks. They are closed to logging and hunting, and they are largely protected from dams, highways, and other such encroachments.

In areas that are part of the National Wilderness Preservation System, whether located in national forests or national parks, the land is protected in its pristine condition. Within definite boundaries set by law, all impact of human activity is kept to a minimum, and no permanent human structures, such as roads, dams, or buildings, are allowed. Logging and the use of mechanized vehicles are against the law. Pursuits that do not scar the land are permitted and, in fact, invited: hiking and backpacking, camping, fishing, cross-country skiing, hunting (except in national parks), and more. Here you will find peace and solitude and relief from the hustle and bustle of everyday life.

One unusual aspect of this book must be mentioned: All distances and area measurements are given in the metric system with the U.S. measures in parentheses. The same is true of temperature: The first figure is in degrees Celsius and the second in degrees Fahrenheit. Thus you should have no difficulty in relating metric values to those of your previous experience. The only exception to the above is that a few short distances are given only in meters, with no equivalent in yards. Because one yard is only slightly less than one meter, we would have been repeating the same figure in most cases.

The contour elevations shown on the maps are expressed in feet to simplify comparison with U.S. Geological Survey (USGS) maps. The contour interval is 250 feet (76 meters).

All distances given in the individual trail descriptions are approximate and should not be taken as the final word. Many trails twist and turn too much for anyone to keep track of them with absolute accuracy, and the convolutions cannot be measured from maps because they do not show up well.

Numbered forest development roads, which generally are well-maintained gravel roads, are abbreviated "FDR" throughout the text.

A word of caution: Do not depend totally on trail signs mentioned in this book. The signs are subject to vandalism by both bears and humans and may have disappeared by the time you get there. Most of the trailheads, though, can still be found because the signposts usually remain standing. You can help by notifying Forest Service personnel about missing trail signs.

There is talk in Forest Service circles about replacing trail names on signs with numbers, in the hope of reducing the incidence of people taking them home as souvenirs. We have attempted to include as many of the numbers as possible.

Finding Your Way in the Woods

When you are hiking in the woods, some method of orientation is necessary. Trail maps are provided for each area covered in this book. Nevertheless, you may want additional information on access roads, private inholdings, or topography.

The U.S. Forest Service issues maps for both George Washington and Jefferson national forests and more detailed maps for many ranger districts within them. These maps carry much useful information on campgrounds and trails. They are also good to have if you are planning to investigate some areas not listed in this guide.

For copies of these maps, write to:
Supervisor
George Washington National Forest
Harrison Plaza
101 N. Main Street, P.O. Box 233
Harrisonburg, VA 22801

Supervisor
Jefferson National Forest
5162 Valleypointe Parkway
Roanoke, VA 24019

For detailed topographic information, the U.S. Geological Survey maps, on a scale of 1:24,000, are available for all areas in the national forests. In addition, the Forest Service now reprints the U.S. Geological Survey maps overlaid with land ownership information. These maps, issued as quadrangles, generally follow latitudes and longitudes, which are conveniently established reference lines. Unfortunately, however, area boundaries rarely coincide with these invented divisions, so you may need two or more adjacent maps to cover the region of your hikes. We have listed all the quadrangles you will need under each area covered in this book.

You can obtain quadrangles from the U.S. Geological Survey, 12201 Sunrise Valley Dr., Reston, VA. Their toll-free telephone number is (800) 872-6227. You can also order an index map of Virginia, which will give you the names of all quadrangles in the state. For Forest Service maps, contact the appropriate forest supervisor's office. Sometimes large-scale maps are available for wilderness areas in the forests.

Contour maps are easy to read once you have mastered the skill. A mountaintop usually appears as a small circle, with the very top marked by a symbol and a figure giving the elevation. Larger contour lines delineate the rest of the mountain, joining all points of equal elevation. The closer the contour lines are to each other, the steeper the hillside. Check the margin of each map for the exact interval between contours, as it may vary from map to map.

On USGS maps, contour lines appear in brown, constructed features are indicated in black or red, streams and water are blue, wooded areas are shaded in green, and clearings are white. Some trails shown may have disappeared since the maps were published, so you may have to retrace your steps or do some bushwhacking.

If you go cross-country—even in areas listed in this guide—

carry a map and compass. Good inexpensive compasses, usually with operating instructions, are available at sporting goods stores. Make sure you know how to use both map and compass before you leave on your trip.

When hiking or bushwhacking, always pay attention to the lay of the land—a stream on the right, a steep hillside on the left, later a clearing on the left and a valley on the right, and so on. This will help you to determine your position on the map and the distance you have covered or have left to hike, as well as to orient yourself in the right direction.

The areas described in this book are hardly big enough to get seriously lost in, but a compass might prove useful nonetheless. If you do not have one and you do get lost, a good rule is to head downhill. Most mountain valleys have a stream; find one and follow it downward. Chances are you will strike a road after some miles.

If you run into serious trouble while hiking, such as an injury to a member of the party, remember that the magic number is three. Blow three times in a row on a whistle; in an open area, spread three ponchos, three shirts, or build three small, smoky fires. Three of anything is the accepted distress call. If your party is large enough, send two or more people for help. But at least one member of the group should stay with the injured person and keep him or her warm while you wait for help to arrive.

(*Editor's note*: The Globe Pequot Press assumes no liability for accidents happening to, or injuries sustained by, readers who engage in the activities described in this book.)

Climate, Terrain, and Equipment

The highest point in the George Washington National Forest is Elliott Knob at 1,361 meters (4,463 feet); in the Jefferson National Forest, Mount Rogers at 1,747 meters (5,729 feet). Mount Rogers is also the highest point in Virginia.

The terrain of Virginia's mountains is varied. Some trails afford easy afternoon hikes; others are steep and rugged. A person in moderately good physical condition should have little trouble negotiating most of these trails. Our trail descriptions will tell you about the exact terrain covered, including the difference in elevation to be negotiated on each trail.

Most regions described in this book lend themselves equally well to day hikes and to weekend backpacking trips. They are relatively small and can be hiked through easily in one day, especially if you have a car shuttle at the other end for one-way hikes. We have also enjoyed packing in a few miles, picking a good campsite, and exploring the surroundings from this base camp.

There are shelters in some areas, especially along the Appalachian Trail, but be prepared to find them already occupied. The AT is one of the most popular trails around. There are also a number of U.S. Forest Service campgrounds scattered throughout the national forests. Some are free; others levy a small fee.

A tent, tarp, or other shelter for the night is good to have along to keep you dry in case the weather turns bad and to protect you from the frequently heavy dew.

If you plan to camp out, select a tent or sleeping site on a higher spot than the surrounding area, even if it is ever so slight. Otherwise you may wake up—as we once did—in a puddle of water. Make sure you get to your campsite while there is plenty of daylight left because the high ground can be hard to spot.

Afternoon showers in the summer are common, particularly at high elevations. It is advisable to carry a poncho or rain jacket on even the brightest summer days, especially if you plan to stay out overnight. A rain jacket can also serve nicely as a windbreaker on an exposed mountaintop or rock outcrop, where you should have something extra to wear when you sit down for lunch after a long, hot hike.

In the winter you will encounter other hazards. Make sure you have *plenty* of warm clothes along; on an exposed peak, the wind-chill factor can get down to dangerous levels. Besides carrying enough clothes to keep you warm, be sure to take lots of food and water. Only through this combination can you expect to maintain your body temperature comfortably.

Hypothermia is a lowering of the core temperature of the body that can be brought on by a lack of any of the above essentials. It can lead to death within two hours. Violent shivering, difficulty in speaking, blue and puffy skin, and erratic movements are hypothermia's warning signs. If you have any of these symptoms, get under shelter immediately. Take off wet clothes and put on more, dry ones—preferably of wool or one of the modern synthetic materials such as polypropylene. Get into your sleeping bag. Drink lots of hot, sweet things, such as coffee or tea with sugar or chocolate. By the way, alcohol is quite the wrong thing to drink. Rather than help, it will aggravate the situation.

Sunburn is possible, especially if there is snow on the ground reflecting the sun's rays. Don't forget your sunglasses, for snow blindness is quite painful.

On the trail, wear a pair of sturdy, comfortable shoes with good traction on the soles. Boots will provide some measure of protection against turned ankles. If you plan to hike a trail with many stream crossings that require wading, you may prefer wearing sneakers, especially if the trail itself is level.

Long treatises have been written on sleeping bags, and there is little we can add. But in the mountains even summer nights can get chilly. Take a bag that is warmer than you think you will need. It's easy to stick an arm or foot out of the bag at night if you get too hot, but it is difficult to compensate for too cold a bag. And you should keep in mind your personal disposition and make allowances for that. If you are a "reptile" and are always cold, as I am, add a few degrees to the low-comfort limit of the sleeping bag supplied by the manufacturer and you should be okay in weather down to the adjusted temperature.

In summer, be sure to take along some kind of headgear—if not a hat, a scarf or bandanna—especially if you are subject to headaches during exposure to bright sun. Although most of the

10

trails described in this book are heavily forested, several are quite open, and there you may need protection. Unfortunately, as the gypsy moth spreads southward, you can expect to find hot sun under the denuded branches of the forest where you had hoped for cool shade.

The Forest Service does not test water regularly and thus cannot identify safe drinking water sources. During most of the year, you can find water in springs or streams at many points along the trails. We do not recommend drinking from streams. We suggest you carry water from a known, safe source. For longer camping trips, where carrying water is not feasible, either bring a water purification kit, chlorine tablets, or boil your water for five minutes. The last option, done in the evening and left standing overnight—covered, of course—should provide cool water for your canteen and the next day's hike.

Hunting is subject to state regulations on all national forest lands. The woods are often overrun with hunters during the deer season. If you can, avoid hiking and camping or backpacking then. If you choose to go anyway, do wear some blaze orange and avoid wearing clothing or packs with white or any light color on them. If in doubt, check with the district ranger's office for advice.

Outdoor Ethics

The most important rule in the out-of-doors is, "If you carry it in full, you can carry it out empty." That applies to all things you use on a hiking, camping, or backpacking trip.

Empty cans should be flattened or crushed. Remove the bottoms and step on them. Flat, they and the lids will occupy practically no space in your pack. If you take soda or beer cans, stomp on them when empty and they will become considerably less bulky. Burying cans is unacceptable because small animals might dig them up and it would take too long for the cans to decompose. A paper or plastic bag comes in handy. Accumulate all your trash in it, and you will have only one item to dispose of when you encounter a trash can back in civilization.

The same pack-out principle, of course, applies to all glass, plastic, and almost every other item invented by humans. And if you want to be better than some of the people who traveled the trail before you, pick up some of the junk they left behind and carry it out, thus leaving the area a bit cleaner than you found it.

If you have a campfire, burn all paper, candy wrappers, and similar things you want to dispose of. Watch out for aluminum foil, though. It won't burn and will have to be packed out with the cans.

Try to keep your campfire small. A large fire consumes a lot of wood, and a big stone ring is unsightly. Remember, too, never to cut living wood for your fire. Usually there is enough dead wood lying about for everybody. And if there is not, so much more the need to burn what little there is sparingly in a small fire. Do not build fires on warm, dry, or windy days. Both Virginia and West Virginia have a fire season in the summer when no open fires are allowed in the woods. Again, check with the district ranger's office for dates and advice.

Using a butane or gasoline stove will also help to conserve wood. In addition, your food will cook faster because the heat concentration under the pot will be greater. It will also save you some work, for wood fires produce awfully sooty pots.

If you do light a fire, douse it well before you leave, then stir the ashes down to the very bottom. Wait a few minutes and stir again. Feel the ashes with your bare hand to make sure they are cold. If hot embers are left on the bottom of the pit, they can slowly burn down to organic matter underneath and start a wildfire.

Try to obliterate all traces of your stay, including the fire ring. Put the stones back where you found them, turning the black side under. Scatter the wet ashes, and cover up the scorched area with pebbles or leaves, if there are any in the immediate vicinity.

When looking for a campsite, you may find the campsites of previous visitors, often recognizable by fire rings. Use one of these established campsites rather than setting up yet another a short distance away.

Avoid congested campsites, whether you are alone or in a group. Plan on having alternative campsites available. You should be able to set up two or even three tents away from the crowd.

Dispose of soapy and dirty used water well away from streams. Dumping it into creeks is unacceptable. In addition to polluting the source of supply, it could be harmful to fellow campers downstream who use the creeks for cooking and drinking.

A word on sanitation: Bury all your wastes. Pick a site well away from any open water—at least 15 meters (50 feet)—and dig a small hole 20 to 25 centimeters (8 to 10 inches) in diameter and no more than 15 to 20 centimeters (6 to 8 inches) deep. Keep the sod intact if possible. After use, fill the hole with the soil and tramp in the sod. Nature will do the rest in a few days. Carrying a small digging tool like a garden trowel is a good idea.

Follow the same procedure for leftover food that you want to dispose of. Black bears do live in the mountains of Virginia, and, although they are shy and normally avoid humans, it is better not to tempt them to come close to a campsite with the smell of unburied food.

Should you decide on a visit to our national forests around the Fourth of July, please remember that this is *not* the place for fireworks. While perhaps appropriate at home or maybe in a city park, the national forests (and national parks) were set aside for peace, quiet, and solitude. In addition to scaring the animals out of their wits, the fireworks could also pose a threat of wildfire during a dry spell.

GEORGE WASHINGTON
NATIONAL FOREST

1
Big Schloss Area

The Big Schloss area, the northernmost part of the George Washington National Forest included in this guidebook, is located mainly in Shenandoah County, Virginia. A substantial portion of the area covered in this chapter actually lies in West Virginia, but as it is all within the same national forest and forms one integral area, we include it here.

The region is generally steep and rugged, with many large rock outcrops that provide spectacular viewpoints above treetops. The most conspicuous of these formations is the Big Schloss itself, on the crest of Mill Mountain, but impressive outcrops exist at many other points. *Schloss* is the German word for castle—the rock outcrops at the Big and Little Schloss probably reminded early settlers of the structures in their homeland. The area contains not only the usual southwest-to-northeast ridges—Mill Mountain and Little Sluice Mountain—but a perpendicular interconnecting ridge formed by Halfmoon Mountain and Sugar Knob.

The Big Schloss area probably was never settled. Iron ore was mined extensively throughout the area in the 1800s—long before the Forest Service even existed, let alone acquired the tract. You can find remains of this activity at Van Buren Furnace on County Road 713. Charcoal was produced from local timber to fuel the furnaces. Trees were cut in an area, then stacked in a small level circle and covered with earth. The wood burned with only small amounts of oxygen to form charcoal, which was then hauled off by horse and wagon to the furnace.

Timbering is still being practiced today at lower altitudes under the multiple-use concept. Clear-cut patches, often quite large, can be seen from some points. The sections that have grown up for a

17

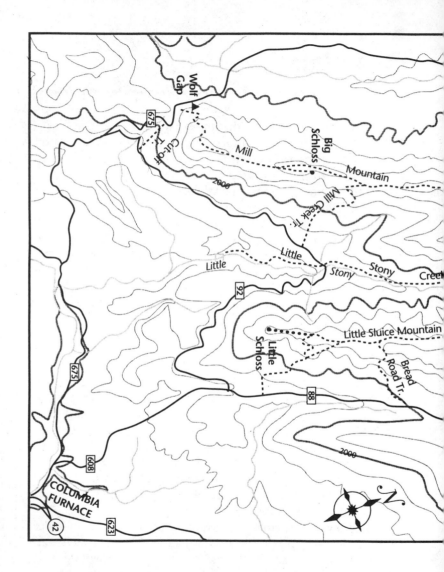

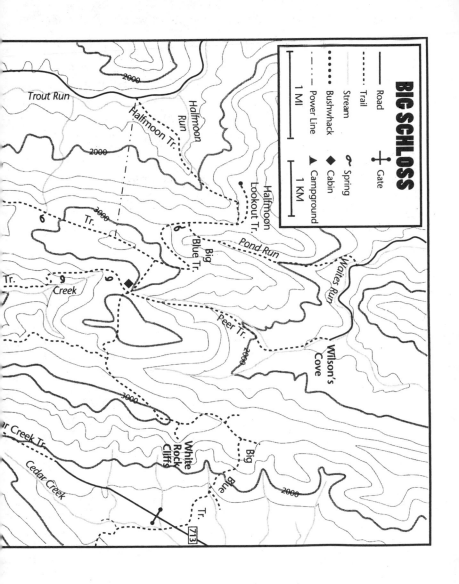

BIG SCHLOSS

Legend:
- Road
- Trail
- Stream
- Bushwhack
- Power Line
- Gate
- Spring
- Cabin
- Campground

1 MI

1 KM

Trout Run

Halfmoon Run

Halfmoon Tr.

Halfmoon Lookout Tr.

Pond Run

Big Blue Tr.

Tr.

Creek

Peer Tr.

Waites Run

Wilson's Cove

Cedar Creek

r Creek Tr.

White Rock Cliffs

Big Blue

Tr.

713

2000

2000

3000

3000

2000

3000

2000

few years may be worth exploring for types of wildlife that avoid heavy forest.

The tree cover is otherwise continuous except at rocky outcrops and a few grassy clearings maintained for the benefit of game. Most of the forest around the summit of Mill Mountain and some of the other high ridges contains a dense understory of mountain laurel. Off-trail travel in these areas consequently is strenuous.

Among wildflowers, the dwarf iris is notably common in late spring, growing in dry, sandy spots beside roads and trails.

Several developments exist in the area. The radio tower on the summit of Mill Mountain has been dismantled, but the power line that runs directly up the west side of the mountain and a building at the top remain. Wolf Gap Campground offers limited car-camping facilities, and the Potomac Appalachian Trail Club maintains a small stone cabin (locked) on the Little Stony Creek Trail near its junction with the Big Blue Trail.

Of great practical benefit to hikers and backpackers are several reliable springs at high elevations. Although there are no designated camping areas for backpackers within the "interior," suitable campsites can be found in a number of places.

All the trails described here except the lower portion of the Peer Trail are on public land. The Peer Trail is posted NO TRESPASSING, but there is an understanding between the owners and the Potomac Appalachian Trail Club, which maintains the trail, to let hikers walk along it. *Please follow the blazes carefully and stay on the trail.* Otherwise, this privilege, which is not an official easement, may be revoked. It is for your own protection, too, as a fierce (biting!) dog guards the farm.

Trail names in the area depend on whose maps and signs you read. In particular, several trails have been linked together to form the "Big Blue Trail." Many of the signs at the trail junctions, however, still bear older trail names. Therefore, when referring to the Big Blue Trail, we also mention its alternate designation. The "Cutoff Trail" from FDR 92 to Wolf Gap Campground is not marked on Forest Service maps.

The Big Schloss area provides some excellent opportunities for circuit hikes, especially if you are willing to walk a couple of miles or so along lightly traveled forest development roads to complete the circuit. Some possibilities for such circuit hikes are:

(1) From Waites Run Road: Up along the Big Blue Trail to the Peer Trail, down the Peer Trail to Waites Run Road, and back along Waites Run Road to the Big Blue Trail (11.9 km; 7.4 mi.).

(2) From FDR 88: Up the Little Sluice Mountain Trail or the Bread Road and Little Sluice Mountain trails, along the Big Blue Trail, and back down the Cedar Run Trail to FDR 88 and your starting point (21.6 km or 17.2 km; 13.4 mi. or 10.7 mi.).

(3) From Wolf Gap Campground: Up Mill Mountain Trail past the Big Schloss, along the Big Blue Trail and down the Little Stony Creek Trail to FDR 92, along FDR 92, then back to the campground via either the Mill Creek and Mill Mountain trails or the abandoned Cut-off Trail (21.1 km; 13.1 mi.).

Maps: USGS Wardensville, Wolf Gap, and Woodstock quadrangles, 7.5 minute series.

MILL MOUNTAIN TRAIL

Length: 9.3 kilometers (5.8 miles)
Direction of travel: North
Difficulty: Moderate
Elevation: 686–1,003 meters (2,250–3,290 feet)
Difference in elevation: 317 meters (1,040 feet)
Markings: Orange blazes
Trail #: 1004
How to get there: Take County Road 675 west from Columbia Furnace to the Wolf Gap Campground (10.6 km; 6.6 mi.). The trail leaves near campsite #9.

The other end of the trail can be reached via the Big Blue Trail.
Trail description: The trail climbs as a jeep road with several switchbacks, ascending 185 m (600 ft.) in 1.2 km (0.8 mi.). It

passes close to but not over the wooded summit at the south end of Mill Mountain. The trail then turns left, decreasing in width to a foot trail, and proceeds northeast along the narrow ridge of the mountain. A right turn along an unmarked trail will lead you to the southern summit of the mountain.

About 50 m past the first rise, you will have some excellent views to the southeast. The trail mostly follows along the west side of the ridge below low rocky cliffs.

At 2.9 km (1.8 mi.) a side trail (white blazes) branches to the right, leading to the top of the ridge and then to the Big Schloss, the largest of the exposed rock formations in this area. After crossing a deep cleft in the rocks on a small wooden footbridge, the side trail ends on the bare rocks of the Big Schloss.

After the side trail branches off for the top of the Big Schloss, the main trail passes below the Big Schloss on the left. It follows the crest of the ridge, with superb views back and up at the Big Schloss.

The junction with the Mill Creek Trail (blazed blue) descending to the right at 3.7 km (2.3 mi.) is well marked. The Mill Mountain Trail continues on straight ahead.

The trail hereafter proceeds slightly below the crest of the ridge, at first mostly on the left and later mostly on the right. Occasional views may be obtained by scrambling up the rocky outcrops along the crest.

After crossing a rocky area at 6.4 km (4 mi.), the trail starts a steady moderate ascent and soon comes to Sandstone Spring (7 km; 4.4 mi.). The abundant clear water and the surrounding grove of hemlocks make this a popular—and often overcrowded—campsite. Treat the water before drinking, as this is an area of heavy human use.

Beyond this spot the trail runs very straight to the northeast, climbing at a moderate rate through a thick patch of mountain laurel. At 8.5 km (5.3 mi.) it passes within a few yards of the summit of Mill Mountain.

The trail now descends moderately as a rough jeep trail, and at 9.3 km (5.8 mi.) it ends at the Big Blue Trail.

HALFMOON TRAIL

Length: 5.2 kilometers (3.2 miles)
Direction of travel: East
Difficulty: Moderate
Elevation: 488–953 meters (1,600-3,125 feet)
Difference in elevation: 465 meters (1,525 feet)
Markings: Yellow blazes
Trail #: 1003

How to get there: From Columbia Furnace, go west on County Road 675, past Wolf Gap Campground. The trailhead is marked by a sign located at 9.7 km (6 mi.) beyond Wolf Gap. This is just at the point where a small power line starts straight up the side of Mill Mountain. This spot may also be reached by driving 12.1 km (7.5 mi.) south from Wardensville, West Virginia, on Trout Run Road. Pay close attention to your odometer and look carefully for the power line as the trailhead is not obvious.

You can reach the opposite end of this trail via the Big Blue Trail.

Trail description: The Halfmoon Trail follows a woods road downhill and over a bridge across Trout Run. A gate blocks the road soon after the bridge.

Continuing on the other side of Trout Run as a woods road, the trail crosses an old overgrown power line clearing and climbs moderately, crossing several rivulets. At about 2.5 km (1.5 mi.), the trail traverses Halfmoon Run just below the junction of a side stream.

The woods road goes downhill from here, but the Halfmoon Trail turns right immediately after the crossing and climbs rather steeply as a foot trail, parallel to Halfmoon Run but well above it.

At one point the trail turns left, going steeply uphill for a few meters, and then turns right again, parallel to its original direction.

At 3.7 km (2.3 mi.) the trail enters a stony ravine and turns sharply right, then climbs steadily, curving to the left.

On the ridgetop, at 4.2 km (2.6 mi.), it joins the Halfmoon Lookout Trail (white blazes). The latter is 1 km (0.6 mi.) long, at first almost level but later starting a gradual ascent until close to its end, where it climbs very steeply to the viewpoint. Here you will find the stone foundations of an old lookout tower and an admirable view up the isolated Trout Run Valley.

At the junction with the trail to the lookout, the Halfmoon Trail turns right and climbs gently along a rounded ridge top. At 5.2 km (3.2 mi.) the Halfmoon Trail ends at the intersection with the Big Blue Trail.

BIG BLUE TRAIL

Length: 14.6 kilometers (9.1 miles)
Direction of travel: Generally south and east
Difficulty: Strenuous
Elevation: 503–945–433 meters (1,650–3,100–1,420 feet)
Difference in elevation: 422–512 meters (1,450–1,680 feet)
Markings: Blue blazes
Trail #: None
How to get there: Take Virginia Route 55 to Wardensville, West Virginia. In Wardensville, take Carpenter Avenue east for about 1.6 km (1 mi.), and turn right onto Waites Run Road just after passing the foot of a long hill—the turn is opposite a sign reading ALLEN HAWKINS COMMUNITY PARK. Go about 8.5 km (5.3 mi.) on Waites Run Road. The trail leaves from the right side of the road, just before the road crosses Waites Run. This section of the trail is also designated "Pond Run Trail."

The Big Blue Trail is a long side spur of the Appalachian Trail and in some places is well maintained and marked. The Big Blue Trail largely follows sections of older trails which bear other names, and signs at trail junctions may indicate either name.
Trail description: The trail starts along the hillside with Pond Run on the left, then it crosses and follows the creek on the other side.

The trail ascends steadily, crossing Pond Run many times. Wading should not be necessary.

During our last visit to the area we found that trail mainte-

24

nance was not up to date: a number of deadfalls required scrambling over, and the trail at times was obscured. These were minor obstacles, though, to an otherwise pleasant hike.

Numerous cascades and many large hemlocks make this section extremely attractive. One hemlock was found to be 3.4 m (11 ft.) in circumference.

The trail now leaves the bottom of the ravine and climbs steeply up a rocky hillside to the right of the stream as a narrow and stony trail. It then climbs at a moderate to easy rate without crossing the stream.

Gradually the trail curves to the right of the ravine, becoming steeper, then climbing more gently. After passing through a fern glade at 3.2 km (2 mi.), it encounters the Halfmoon Trail coming in from the right. At this point the Big Blue Trail turns left.

After turning left, the trail crosses a small stream, the headwaters of Halfmoon Run, and shortly afterward passes near the spring that is its ultimate source.

A realigned section of the Big Blue Trail starts to ascend Mill Mountain toward the north. The trail here is a primitive foot path, rough and rocky in spots. After coming to an overlook at a clearing in Wilson's Cove, the trail turns back south, still climbing gently, to its junction with the Mill Mountain Trail. At this intersection the Big Blue Trail turns left and the Mill Mountain Trail runs straight ahead.

The Big Blue Trail continues as a jeep trail, passing many large anthills and descending through scrubby woods to a saddle at 6.3 km (3.9 mi.) At this point the Peer Trail leaves left and the Little Stony Creek Trail leaves right. A few meters down the Little Stony Creek Trail you will find the Sugar Knob Cabin and, in a short while, a spring.

From the saddle the Big Blue Trail goes straight ahead uphill and passes over a shoulder of Sugar Knob, with attractive open woods. It descends, at first moderately, later rather steeply, and at 7.8 km (4.8 mi.) meets the Little Sluice Mountain Trail coming in as a jeep trail from the right.

From this junction the Big Blue Trail first continues straight ahead as a foot trail and then turns to the left. It climbs at a moderate rate along the west side of Little Sluice Mountain, passing a good viewpoint into Racer Camp Hollow on the left. It runs next along the broad ridge of the mountain, passing through scrubby oaks.

At 9.6 km (6 mi.), at a sign indicating VIEW 0.5 KM (0.3 MI.), a small trail (white blazes) winds downhill to the right to White Rock Cliffs, with fine views first to the south and, at the end of the trail, to the north.

Shortly after the departure of this side trail, the Big Blue Trail passes a long, low, rocky wall on the left. Afterward it briefly falls steeply from the top of the ridge, levels off again, and at 10.5 km (6.5 mi.) comes to a jeep trail.

Here the Big Blue Trail turns right along the jeep trail. Lupines grow in and near the trail at this point.

After roughly 0.6 km (0.4 mi.) on the jeep trail, the Big Blue Trail turns right as a foot trail, descending at an increasingly steep rate. The jeep trail continues straight ahead and ends at a recent clear-cut. If you follow a logging road from the clear-cut, you will get to the four-way intersection mentioned at the beginning of the Cedar Creek Trail.

About 0.5 km (0.3 mi.) from the jeep trail, the Big Blue Trail bears left, while an abandoned trail drops steeply straight ahead.

The Big Blue Trail now goes steeply down a ridge and enters a broad, dry ravine. The footpath is faint here, but the trail is well blazed. The trail ascends slightly and then descends past large boulders into another ravine, which it follows downward.

After passing through a small clearing—a good campsite with water close by—the trail becomes much wider and runs beside a small stream on the right.

At 12.5 km (7.8 mi.) the Big Blue Trail turns right *(watch carefully for this)* and crosses the stream, while a wider trail goes straight ahead. This road leads to private land.

After fording the stream, the trail climbs the far bank and then drops gradually, skirting a grassy game clearing on the left. The trail now goes straight across a wide forest development road. At 13.7 km (8.5 mi.) the trail turns right, heading upstream beside Cedar Creek, which it soon crosses. After the crossing, which can be made on stones with care, the trail becomes muddy. This section of the trail is rather poorly marked.

Shortly after reaching the end of a wet section, the trail forks at 14.6 km (9.1 mi.). From this point the Big Blue Trail, the left fork, ascends Little North Mountain and follows its almost level ridge to the northeast, out of the Big Schloss area, and eventually reaches County Road 600 at Fetzer Gap.

The right fork is the former alignment of the Cedar Creek Trail, and leads to Forest Development Road 88.

PEER TRAIL

Length: 5.3 kilometers (3.3 miles)
Direction of travel: North
Difficulty: Easy
Elevation: 915–519 meters (3,000–1,700 feet)
Difference in elevation: 396 meters (1,300 feet)
Markings: Purple blazes
Trail #: 1002
How to get there: Via the Big Blue Trail or, to hike the trail in the opposite direction from Wardensville, West Virginia, take Carpenter Avenue 1.6 km (1 mi.) and turn right onto Waites Run Road. Go 10.1 km (6.3 mi.) to the point where a large gate marks the beginning of private land. A few parking spaces are available just outside the gate.
Trail description: The Peer Trail starts from the Big Blue Trail in the saddle between Mill Mountain and Sugar Knob, opposite the trailhead for the Little Stony Creek Trail.

The trail descends steadily along the side of a ravine well above Waites Run, which flows at the bottom. At first it is only a foot trail, but lower down it becomes an old unused woods road, wide and smooth.

The forest is attractive and open, with a mossy floor.

At 3 km (1.9 mi.), the trail approaches a large meadow on the right and skirts around two sides of it. A NO TRESPASSING sign will indicate the beginning of private land. The owners have privately agreed to let hikers cross it. Please stick closely to the blazed trail and avoid straying onto the rest of the property—their dog has been known to bite trespassers.

The trail goes along a dirt road, mostly through woods, and crosses a stream on a washed-out concrete bridge. At 4.2 km (2.6 mi.) it comes to another meadow with a shed for farm machinery. Here the trail *(watch the purple blazes)* leaves the road and turns right into the woods. Within 50 meters it meets a faint car track, and afterward turns left again.

The Peer Trail continues through woods. It then enters another meadow, skirting along the right edge—continue to watch for blazes.

After crossing a wooden bridge near a group of farm buildings, the trail joins a dirt road. It then crosses a concrete bridge and turns left to go through a gate onto Waites Run Road. At 5.3 km (3.3 mi.) it passes a large reservoir pond on the left.

Be sure to close all gates behind you so that farm animals will not wander away.

From the gate it is 1.6 km (1 mi.) left along Waites Run Road to the foot of the Big Blue Trail (Pond Run section).

MILL CREEK TRAIL

Length: 2.4 kilometers (1.5 miles)
Direction of travel: Northwest
Difficulty: Strenuous
Elevation: 491–839 meters (1,610–2,750 feet)
Difference in elevation: 348 meters (1,140 feet)

Markings: Blue blazes
Trail #: 415
How to get there: Via Forest Development Road 92, following directions to Little Stony Creek Trail. From Little Stony Creek, continue west on FDR 92 for 0.6 km (0.4 mi.). The trail leaves to the right, climbing over the low road bank in the middle of a gentle curve to the right. The trailhead is marked by blue blazes on trees and rocks. The other end can be reached via the Mill Mountain Trail.
Trail description: The Mill Creek Trail climbs moderately as a woods road. It dips briefly and enters a broad, rocky gully.

After crossing to the other side of the gully, the trail ascends steeply below a giant stone wall. It follows a broad, gently rounded ridge.

At 1.4 km (0.9 mi.), just after you have passed over the ridge, the trail makes a switchback and recrosses the ridge. It traverses a region of lichen-covered rocks.

The trail now enters a shallow ravine where the ground is covered with loose stones; then it switches back again.

Shortly after this second switchback, the boulders 30 m to the right of the trail offer a dramatic valley view.

At 2.4 km (1.5 mi.) the trail reaches the Mill Mountain Trail at the mountain's ridge. A small cairn marks the spot. From here it is about 0.8 km (0.5 mi.) south along the Mill Mountain Trail to the Big Schloss.

LITTLE STONY CREEK TRAIL

Length: 7.7 kilometers (4.8 miles)
Direction of travel: South
Difficulty: Moderate
Elevation: 915–397 meters (3,000–1,300 feet)
Difference in elevation: 518 meters (1,700 feet)
Markings: Yellow blazes
Trail #: 57

How to get there: Via the Big Blue Trail. To hike the trail in a northerly direction, take County Road 675 west from Columbia Furnace for 0.8 km (0.5 mi.) and turn right onto County Road 608, which soon becomes Forest Development Road 88. At 3.7 km (2.3 mi.) turn left on FDR 92, and go 5.3 km (3.3 mi.) to the crossing of Little Stony Creek. The trail crosses the road there.

Trail description: Little Stony Creek Trail starts on the Big Blue Trail at the saddle between Mill Mountain and Sugar Knob, opposite the Peer Trail.

About 50 m downhill, it passes the small Sugar Knob Cabin, which is maintained by the Potomac Appalachian Trail Club. The cabin is locked (for reservations see Introduction).

After another 50 m, the trail passes a spring on the left.

The trail descends beside the stream, crossing once after about 100 m and again after about 0.2 km (0.1 mi.) It then enters a field of rocks with an underground stream that is audible but usually not visible. The slope is entirely forested with relatively open woods.

Descending along the side of a steep hill, the trail passes another spring at 1.6 km (1 mi.). If you hike this trail during or shortly after a good rain, you may find yourself walking in a secondary stream next to the real one, so come prepared for wet feet.

Soon thereafter the trail's descent is moderated by two switchbacks. At the second switchback, the foot trail changes to a rough jeep trail, which, after about 20 m, crosses a small stream. After an additional 100 m it passes another spring.

Here the trail runs mostly about 100 m above Little Stony Creek, but later it descends to the stream, crossing a small tributary and passing in some places through dense growths of hemlock. It continues near the west bank of the stream until it crosses Little Stony Creek Road, FDR 92, at 5.5 km (3.4 mi.) from the start.

On the other side of Little Stony Creek Road, the trail continues as a broad woods road. Within 100 m it crosses a small tributary of Little Stony Creek. Here a side trail to the left leads to a beautiful view of the creek, with clear water flowing between mossy rocks, heavily shaded by large hemlocks.

At 6.9 km (4.3 mi.) a side road, which eventually becomes lost in the tangled vegetation, leaves to the right, and the Little Stony Creek Trail continues straight ahead.

The trail now passes an area of huge jumbled rocks on the right, with a small stream running beneath them. It then leads through a hemlock grove, with a side road branching left to the stream bank while the main trail continues to the right, passing below a high vertical cliff.

Soon thereafter, at 7.7 km (4.8 mi.), the trail reaches the Woodstock Reservoir. Beyond this point the trail leaves the national forest and enters private land. Please respect property rights and retrace your steps.

LITTLE SLUICE MOUNTAIN TRAIL

Length: 6.9 kilometers (4.3 miles)
Direction of travel: North
Difficulty: Moderate
Elevation: 476–820 meters (1,560–2,690 feet)
Difference in elevation: 344 meters (1,130 feet)
Markings: Purple blazes
Trail #: 401
How to get there: From Columbia Furnace, take County Road 675 west about 0.8 km (0.5 mi.) to County Road 608, which leaves uphill to the right. Follow 608, which becomes Forest Development Road 88. At 3.7 km (2.3 mi.) FDR 92 leaves to the left. Continue straight ahead on FDR 88. The Little Sluice Mountain Trail begins on the left, 0.8 km (0.5 mi.) beyond the junction with FDR 92.
Trail description: The Little Sluice Mountain Trail is a rough road that first ascends at a moderate rate and then at 0.5 km (0.3 mi.) from the trailhead turns right, climbing more steeply. At 1.4 km (0.9 mi.) from the start, the trail forks.

The right branch, which is 0.6 km (0.4 mi.) shorter, ascends along the side of the mountain, starting as a little-used jeep trail and later narrowing to a foot trail. Where this foot trail seems to diminish to nothing, the left fork of the trail can be rejoined by cutting through the woods to the ridge top a few meters away. If you are not planning a side trip to the Little Schloss, you may wish to take this branch of the trail.

From the fork the left branch of the trail ascends steeply via switchbacks to the summit ridge of Little Sluice Mountain. Where it reaches the summit, at 2.1 km (1.3 mi.), there is a grassy game clearing containing a few isolated spruces.

From this clearing a side trip south to the Little Schloss can be made. A trail has become established through frequent usage. Head straight across the meadow and into the woods on the opposite side, following the ridge crest to the southwest. Pass over one small rise, descend to a saddle, and then scramble up the rocks to the large white cliffs of the Little Schloss, about 500 m after leaving the meadow. *Caution* is required because of many loose stones and rocks on the Little Schloss, but the views from the top are spectacular.

Returning to the meadow and rejoining the left fork of the Little Sluice Mountain Trail, you travel along the summit ridge of Little Sluice Mountain, almost level at first and then passing over a knob about 30 m high.

After descending on the far side of this knob, the trail crosses a short level spot with large oak trees. Just where the trail curves to the left and starts downhill, at 3.4 km (2.1 mi.), you will see the Bread Road Trail leaving to the right.

After this junction, the Little Sluice Mountain Trail passes a clearing on the left, from which you obtain a nice view of the Big Schloss, 3.2 km (2 mi.) away as the crow flies but much farther as the hiker strides.

The trail then slowly descends the left flank of the ridge of Little Sluice Mountain. After passing over two saddles that join the main ridge to outlying knobs, a short side trail to the right leads to a spring at 5.3 km (3.3 mi.).

After crossing another saddle, the trail descends, turns left and then right, and crosses a stream that may run year-round.

The trail then ascends moderately until at 6.9 km (4.3 mi.) it ends at the Big Blue Trail.

BREAD ROAD TRAIL

Length: 1.6 kilometers (1 mile)
Direction of travel: West
Difficulty: Moderate
Elevation: 589–796 meters (1,930–2,610 feet)
Difference in elevation: 207 meters (680 feet)
Markings: Red blazes
Trail #: 411
How to get there: From Columbia Furnace take County Road 675 west for 0.8 km (0.5 mi.) and turn right onto County Road 608, which soon becomes Forest Development Road 88. Continue 3.4 km (2.1 mi.) on FDR 88 beyond its junction with FDR 92 and park at a small turnout just past the trailhead. You can reach the other end of the trail via the Little Sluice Mountain Trail.
Trail description: The trail, providing an alternate route to the top of Little Sluice Mountain, starts about 0.3 km (0.2 mi.) before the point where FDR 88 is chained off.

Follow a rough road about 60 paces uphill and, at the spot where it forks, curve around sharply to the left.

Continuing uphill on a moderate slope, the trail first is mossy, then becomes steeper and rougher. You may find water in the trail here after wet weather. This, together with a rocky and somewhat eroded trail, can make walking difficult, especially if you are trying to keep your feet dry. The trail is beautiful, though, and the trees provide nice shade during the summer months.

The trail curves to the right and heads steeply up the hill, continuing through young trees and then entering older growth. The footing is poor here, with loose stones on the steep slope, but the trail soon improves as it curves to the left and becomes less steep.

Finally it turns to the right and climbs again more steeply for about 100 m to Little Sluice Mountain Trail on the ridge of the mountain.

CEDAR CREEK TRAIL

Length: 5.1 kilometers (3.2 miles)
Direction of travel: Southwest
Difficulty: Easy
Elevation: 412–625 meters (1,350–2,050 feet)
Difference in elevation: 213 meters (700 feet)
Markings: Yellow blazes
Trail #: 573

How to get there: From Van Buren Furnace or, to hike the trail in the opposite direction, from the end of Forest Development Road 88. To reach Van Buren Furnace from Columbia Furnace, go north 12.7 km (7.9 mi.) on County Road 623 to County Road 600 and turn left, crossing over North Mountain at Fetzer Gap. After 7.1 km (4.4 mi.) on 600, turn left on County Road 603 and go 1.9 km (1.2 mi.) to County Road 713. Continue straight on 713, pass the ruins of Van Buren Furnace, and enter the national forest where the road is gated. You will then come to what looks like a four-way intersection. The right turn leads to a recent clear-cut, the left turn goes to Cedar Creek, a few meters away, and a gate. The road straight ahead is the beginning of the Cedar Creek Trail. You can either park here at the side of the road or continue straight ahead, past the junction with the Big Blue Trail, and park at a Forest Service gate.

To reach the end of FDR 88, go 0.8 km (0.5 mi.) west from Columbia Furnace on County Road 675 to County Road 608. Turn right on 608, which soon becomes FDR 88, and continue to its end. Here is a traffic circle type of turnaround for your car.

Trail description: Walk up the road past the point where the Big Blue Trail crosses it and continue to follow it past the gate. It travels along a hillside a fair distance from Cedar Creek itself, passing at one point over a small saddle. Some old mines can be seen in the hillside.

The trail was rerouted a while back because the old woods road beside the creek is often almost as wet as the creek itself. In fact, we once found the nest of a Louisiana waterthrush not in the bank of the creek, where it might be expected, but in the bank of the trail.

After keeping to the hillside for a while, the trail approaches closer to the creek. Shortly thereafter it becomes a foot trail.

Continue following the yellow blazes. Eventually, the trail joins the old road next to Cedar Creek and follows it to the gate and the traffic circle on FDR 88 beyond.

If you do not mind possible wet feet, you can follow the Big Blue Trail down to the creek and hike up the old road beside it. The road is becoming quite overgrown and has many fallen trees, which make it a slow hike. You will eventually be joined by the actual trail, with its yellow blazes.

CUT-OFF TRAIL

Length: 0.6 kilometer (0.4 mile)
Direction of travel: Northwest
Difficulty: Moderate
Elevation: 549–650 meters (1,800–2,130 feet)
Difference in elevation: 101 meters (330 feet)
Markings: None
Trail #: None
How to get there: The base of the trail is located on Forest Development Road 92, 4.5 km (2.8 mi.) west of the point where the road crosses Little Stony Creek. The trail starts up the hillside just where the road begins to run slightly downhill into a ravine, where it makes a switchback.

The other end of the trail is just below Wolf Gap Campground on Route 675. You may have to look carefully for the junction.

Trail description: Once it's found, this trail is easily followed, as it is an old roadbed cut deeply into the hillside.

The trail has not been maintained in recent years, but vegetation has not yet totally reclaimed it.

The ascent toward County Road 675 is quite steep, and the trail meets 675 just below Wolf Gap Campground.

2
Laurel Fork Area

The Laurel Fork area is a high-altitude region in the northwestern corner of Highland County, bordered on the north and west by West Virginia. The Laurel Fork, the stream that gives the region its name, flows from south to north, bisecting it. In the eastern section is Middle Mountain, a narrow ridge that parallels the Laurel Fork. The western section consists of fingerlike ridges that point toward the Laurel Fork. Between these ridges, six tributaries flow eastward into the main stream, and trails follow four of them. The main attraction of the area is its relative remoteness and gentle beauty.

Around the turn of the century the land in the Laurel Fork area was owned by the Norfolk and Western Railroad. The company logged it and hauled the timber out via narrow-gauge railroads that ran along the slopes above the streams. The railbeds, stripped of hardware, still exist, and their gentle grades form the basis of much of the trail system.

The U.S. Forest Service purchased the land in 1922. Since then the forest has regenerated, with only a modest amount of thinning being done by the agency. It now is a fine example of a young northern hardwood forest.

At almost all headwaters you can find beaver ponds and meadows. In fact, you can't miss them! Dawn and dusk are good times to watch beavers at work. If you are lucky, you may see a snowshoe hare, mink, or muskrat. Streams are stocked with brook trout and support some native trout.

The trees most commonly seen are red spruce, hemlock, white pine, and red maple at high elevations, and northern red oak, sugar maple, beech, yellow and sweet (black) birch, and black cherry throughout the rest of the area. Rhododendron and moun-

37

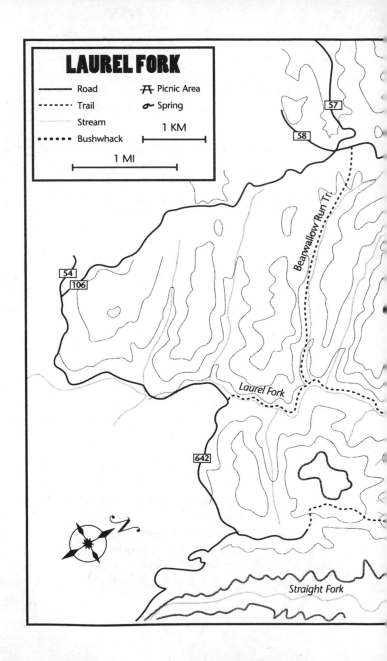

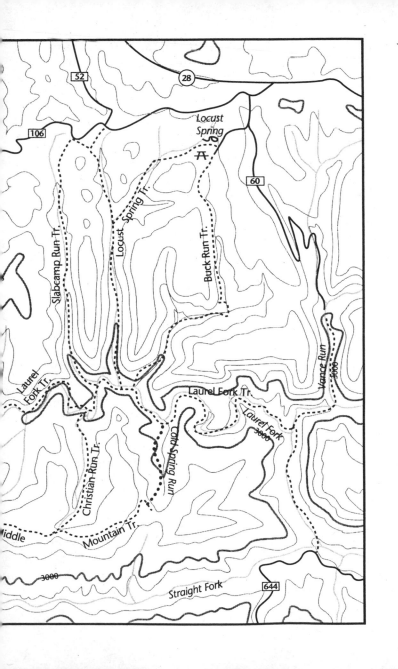

tain laurel are most conspicuous close to the Laurel Fork. Greenbrier, wintergreen, aster, goldenrod, mosses, ferns, and an abundance of other plants, as well as mushrooms, round out the inventory. In some spots berry bushes grow.

The only developed campsite is Locust Spring Picnic Area in the northern corner. This site is accessible by dirt road and features picnic tables, fire rings, a three-sided shelter, a spring, and vault toilets. There are abundant campsites along the Laurel Fork.

The beaver meadows in the upper reaches of the tributaries are tempting campsites. They are fragile and get trampled easily, however, besides often being wet, so try to find a campsite in the woods instead.

The Forest Service claims there are 45.9 kilometers (28.5 miles) of trails in the Laurel Fork area. But most trails are, to say the least, informal. That's all right as long as you are forewarned to expect a little bushwhacking. The forest understory is sparse, and bushwhacking is not difficult. Only in the rhododendron thickets along the Laurel Fork can you get really tangled up if you lose the trail. But even they are manageable with a few short detours.

Most of the trailheads and junctions are well marked. In between the markers, you need imagination. The Forest Service has done little trail work, while the beavers have done quite a lot. Trails in the upper reaches of the tributaries near the beaver meadows tend to meander and disappear. The best procedure seems to be to stick fairly close to the hillsides while bypassing the beaver ponds and look for game trails and railroad grades that are going your way. This has the added advantage of lessening human impact on the meadows. Carry a topographic map and keep your eye on the ridge tops and streams as landmarks.

Farther down the tributaries the valleys narrow, the beaver ponds disappear, and you can pick up a real trail or railroad grade that leads to the bottom. The old railroad grades make excellent trails when they go where you want to go. Many of them, however, tend to creep higher and higher on the hillsides or even to disappear. The solution, then, is to bushwhack down to the nearest stream, where you usually can find a fisherman's trail, a game trail, or another railroad grade.

The trail along the Laurel Fork is good, but it crosses the stream a number of times. Upstream, wading is not needed, except perhaps when the water is very high. Downstream from the Slabcamp Run Trail junction, it is necessary to wade across.

The Laurel Fork Trail and the Middle Mountain Trail cross private land for short distances (see trail descriptions). Be considerate and don't abuse the privilege of passage. All other trails are on public land.

The Laurel Fork area offers many possibilities for circuit hikes. All trails in the western section are connected at the top by Forest Development Road 106 and at the bottom by the Laurel Fork Trail. The shortest circuit, Buck Run to Locust Spring, is about 9.7 kilometers (6 miles) long, starting and ending at the Locust Spring Picnic Area. For most other circuits you will have to walk along FDR 106 or FDR 60 for part of the way, and that can be somewhat boring. But you should examine the map and make up your own circuit hike.

The Locust Spring Picnic Area is a good starting point from which to reach the trails. To get to the picnic area from the south, go west from Monterey on U.S. 250 for 33.8 kilometers (21 miles), and turn sharply right onto West Virginia Route 28. Go 10.8 kilometers (6.7 miles), and turn right onto a dirt road marked LOCUST SPRING PICNIC AREA. After 0.8 kilometers (0.5 miles) turn left at the first intersection (Allegheny Road—FDR 106—goes right). Bear right at the second intersection (FDR 60 goes left) to the picnic ground.

From the north, take U.S. 33 west from Harrisonburg through Franklin, West Virginia. At 22.5 kilometers (14 miles) past Franklin, turn left onto West Virginia Route 28. From there it is 25.7 kilometers (16 miles) to the turnoff on the left marked LOCUST SPRING PICNIC AREA. Follow above directions to the picnic area.

Maps: USGS Thornwood and Snowy Mountain quadrangles, 7.5 minute series; Warm Springs Ranger District map, George Washington National Forest.

LAUREL FORK TRAIL

Length: 14.5 kilometers (9 miles)
Direction of travel: Generally south
Difficulty: Moderate to easy
Elevation: 904–970 meters (2,965–3,180 feet)
Difference in elevation: 66 meters (215 feet)
Markings: Blue blazes
Trail #: 450
How to get there: From the Locust Spring Picnic Area, take Forest Development Road 60 downhill, via switchbacks, to the point where it ends beside Vance Run. The trail runs from there down Vance Run.

If you wish to hike the trail in the opposite direction, go south on FDR 106 to its junction with County Road 642, and turn left. At 1.6 km (1 mi.) after 642 crosses the Laurel Fork, a dirt road turns back on the left, with a marker for the Laurel Fork Trail. Park on County Road 642 and do not drive down the dirt road, which leads to private property.

Trail description: The trail, an old woods road closed to motorized vehicles, follows Vance Run east through thick woods. It descends gently in the steep-sided valley.

At the confluence of Vance and Sam's runs, the trail turns south; a little later it returns east.

At 2.4 km (1.5 mi.) Vance Run flows into the Laurel Fork. (The old woods road continues downstream 1.9 km [1.2 mi.] along the Laurel Fork to meet County Road 644 at the confluence of the Laurel Fork and Straight Fork. Beyond this point, the river is called the North Fork of the South Branch of the Potomac River.)

Back at the place where Vance Run flows into the Laurel Fork, turn right (south) onto the actual trail along the Laurel Fork. The trail is now a footpath, following the Laurel Fork upstream. It is rather level and easy hiking, but be prepared to wade across the stream on numerous occasions.

Shortly after you have begun hiking up the Laurel Fork, you

will come to a beautiful cliff rising straight up out of the river on the left bank.

In a few places the trail is overgrown with rhododendron, but this is nothing to worry about. You can still follow the path through the thickets by bending over a little and parting the branches with your hands.

You will find some grassy clearings beside the river. In a few, old apple trees are growing. The fruit is small and a bit on the sour side, but you may enjoy picking and eating some anyway during the fall.

The Laurel Fork has attractive swimming holes in a few places. Occasional rocky bluffs make for scenic hiking.

At 6 km (3.7 mi.) you will see Cold Spring Run joining the Laurel Fork on the left. Shortly thereafter, Buck Run flows into the river on the right. From here the trail will be quite obvious—again an old woods road—and the stream crossings usually can be negotiated without wading, although conditions vary with the water level.

A good number of streams flow into the Laurel Fork at short intervals, with trails following most of them. Some intervals, from stream to stream, are:

Cold Spring Run to Buck Run	1.1 km (0.7 mi.)
Buck Run to Locust Spring Run	0.5 km (0.3 mi.)
Locust Spring Run to Slabcamp Run	0.5 km (0.3 mi.)
Slabcamp Run to Christian Run	0.8 km (0.5 mi.)
Christian Run to Bearwallow Run	3.9 km (2.4 mi.)

The Laurel Fork Trail winds its way along the river valley, always staying close to the stream. The turns and twists are quite scenic, and the hiking is easy.

At 12.7 km (7.9 mi.), near the confluence of Laurel Fork and Bearwallow Run, there is a flat open area with a beaver pond right on the Laurel Fork. Some of it has become meadowlike but is still rather soggy. Tread carefully if you venture here, or you will have wet feet in no time. The beaver dam was in good repair when we were there last.

At 14.3 km (8.9 mi.) you will reach the end of the national forest property. Cross the stream for the last time, and you will find a cabin on your left. The land around it is privately owned, but the Forest Service has an agreement with the owners whereby they permit access to the Laurel Fork. Make sure you stay on the dirt road, and do not stray onto the private property. If the access privilege is abused, it will be revoked.

The trail ends at 14.5 km (9 mi.) on County Road 642.

BUCK RUN TRAIL

Length: 4 kilometers (2.5 miles)
Direction of travel: Southeast
Difficulty: Moderate
Elevation: 869–1,159 meters (2,850–3,800 feet)
Difference in elevation: 290 meters (950 feet)
Markings: Blue blazes
Trail #: 598
How to get there: The trail starts at the Locust Spring Picnic Area. The other end of the trail can be reached via the Laurel Fork Trail.
Trail description: Buck Run Trail begins just east of the parking area for the Locust Spring Picnic Area. Bear right on a gated two-track trail, which may have been an old railroad grade or logging road. Follow it for about 0.8 km (0.5 mi.) through woods along the side of a hill. To your left (north) you will see beaver ponds and meadows.

In a low saddle, just past a good view of beaver ponds, the trail forks. Take the left branch—not too obvious—down through open woods towards the stream.

Going downhill from the saddle, the trail meanders along the edge of more beaver ponds and among meadows and spruces. You can see a lot of birds here.

Eventually the trail merges with another railroad grade that comes in from the right (south). Follow this grade for 1.3 km (0.8

mi.) along the north side of Buck Knob. Buck Run drops farther below to your left.

Just before you reach the eastern end of Buck Knob, where the railroad grade turns the corner to the right, the trail forks again. The Buck Run Trail goes left as a narrow footpath, dropping off the railroad grade and descending by switchbacks to Buck Run. This split from the railroad grade is ill defined, but there is a forked tree in the middle of the division. If you notice the railroad grade turning right (south) around the end of Buck Knob, you have gone about 30 m too far.

At the bottom of the switchbacks, the trail crosses Buck Run to the north side, follows the bank for a short distance, and then recrosses to the south bank at the spot where the stream turns southward. These are the only stream crossings along this trail, and they do not require wading.

From the second crossing of Buck Run, it is 1.9 km (1.2 mi.) to the Laurel Fork. The trail follows the west bank, remaining close to Buck Run. You will find a trail marker at the junction with the Laurel Fork Trail, only a short distance from the Laurel Fork. There are a number of good campsites nearby.

LOCUST SPRING TRAIL

Length: 5.6 kilometers (3.5 miles)
Direction of travel: Southeast
Difficulty: Moderate
Elevation: 873–1,159 meters (2,862–3,800 feet)
Difference in elevation: 286 meters (938 feet)
Markings: Blue blazes
Trail #s: 633 and 633A
How to get there: This trail has three trailheads. Approach 1, which is the easiest to follow, begins at the Locust Spring Picnic Area. Approach 2, which requires a bit more imagination, begins opposite Forest Development Road 52 along FDR 106, 2.1 km (1.3 mi.) south

of the road to the picnic area. A blue blaze marks the spot. Approach 3 begins at the Slabcamp Run trailhead. Follow the blue blazes to the left.

You can reach the opposite end of the trail via the Laurel Fork Trail.

Trail description: For Approach 1: Walk from the Locust Spring Picnic Area toward the spring and you will see the trailhead to your left, before you drop down to the spring. The trail is *not* open to motorized vehicles of any kind, including trail bikes.

For 1.3 km (0.8 mi.) the trail is easy to follow, leading through hemlocks and white pines, most of which obviously have been planted; then it forks, the right branch going down to Locust Spring Run. Take the narrower left branch through more evergreen forest. The trail eventually drops down to the stream and crosses it several times. Continue through open, not-too-brushy bottom-land, crossing and recrossing the stream.

Near a stand of red pine on the hill to your left (northeast), you will come to the junction with the second approach to Locust Spring Trail. Cross to the south side of the stream.

For Approach 2: Leave FDR 106 and head down through the woods for 50 m until you reach Locust Spring Run. Keep generally to the right (south) of the creek.

After following the stream for 150 m you will begin to encounter a series of beaver ponds. Keep to the south of them, following the trail or game trails, or bushwhacking, as necessary. At the bottom of the chain of beaver ponds is a marshy area, from which the trail eventually emerges. It becomes a railroad grade along the south side of the stream.

Look for a valley coming in from the north and the junction with Approach 1 to Locust Spring Trail at 2.7 km (1.7 mi.).

For Approach 3: Start at the trailhead for the Slabcamp Run Trail and take the trail that leaves immediately downhill to the left. After a few hundred meters this trail joins the second approach to the Locust Spring Trail.

After the junction, the combined trails follow the railroad

grade intermittently. The path crosses the stream several times, but no wading is necessary. The forest is open.

After the final stream crossing, the valley narrows. The trail becomes a railroad grade, following the north bank of the stream for the remaining distance.

You will find a marker at the end of the trail, near the Laurel Fork. Just to the south is a fire ring. Many good campsites are available.

SLABCAMP RUN TRAIL

Length: 4 kilometers (2.5 miles)
Direction of travel: Southeast
Difficulty: Moderate
Elevation: 885–1,112 meters (2,900–3,650 feet)
Difference in elevation: 228 meters (750 feet)
Markings: Blue blazes
Trail #: 600
How to get there: Go south on Forest Development Road 106 for 2.7 km (1.7 mi.) past the road to the Locust Spring Picnic Area and park near the sign marking the trailhead.

The opposite end of the trail can be reached via the Laurel Fork Trail.

Trail description: The trail forks 30 m from the trailhead; take the right fork at the gate and follow it down a gentle hill. The left fork leads to the Locust Spring Trail.

You will pass a second gate. The trail levels off, winding through a meadow and skirting the inevitable series of beaver ponds. It then narrows to a foot trail and becomes rather difficult to follow.

Once past the beaver ponds, the trail follows Slabcamp Run and crosses it numerous times. Be on the alert! Much of the best trail is on the north side of the stream, but it runs up and down the side of the hill. In many places it hardly seems to exist. The going can be treacherous, especially if the rocks are wet. For the last kilometer (0.6 mi.) you will probably have to walk down the broad, gently sloping streambed. No difficulties here, except during high water.

There are some interesting rock formations along the way, green and gray sandstone and shale. This is a good place for rock hounds to stop for a look around.

At trail's end, the junction with the Laurel Fork Trail is marked by a sign.

To reach the main part of the Laurel Fork Trail, you must cross to the east side of the Laurel Fork, and wading probably will be necessary.

BEARWALLOW RUN TRAIL

Length: 4 kilometers (2.5 miles)
Direction of travel: Southeast
Difficulty: Moderate
Elevation: 961–1,129 meters (3,150–3,700 feet)
Difference in elevation: 168 meters (550 feet)
Markings: Blue blazes
Trail #: 601
How to get there: Take Forest Development Road 106 south for 6.3 km (3.9 mi.) past the road to the Locust Spring Picnic Area and park at the sign marking the trailhead.

You can reach the opposite end of the trail via the Laurel Fork Trail.

Trail description: From the trailhead, follow the trail until it disappears into beaver ponds and meadows along Bearwallow Run.

Here you will have to be a little ingenious to avoid wet feet. Your best strategy is to stay to the right (south) of the beaver ponds, keeping on the side of the hill. Follow game trails and old logging or railroad grades wherever possible. Expect to do some bushwhacking.

The scenic views redeem this trail. There are beautiful vistas over open meadows with ferns and scattered spruces. It's worth the scrambling.

About 1.6 km (1 mi.) down the valley, on the south side in a stand of hemlocks, you will arrive at a good railroad grade. It can be followed the rest of the way down Bearwallow Run to the Laurel Fork.

The trail junction with the Laurel Fork Trail is marked by a signpost near the Laurel Fork. There are good campsites nearby.

MIDDLE MOUNTAIN TRAIL

Length: 4.3 kilometers (2.7 miles)
Direction of travel: Northeast
Difficulty: Easy to moderate
Elevation: 1,154–1,190 meters (3,784–3,901 feet)
Difference in elevation: 36 meters (117 feet)
Markings: Blue blazes
Trail #: 457
How to get there: From the Locust Spring Picnic Area, drive south on Forest Development Road 106 to its junction with County Road 642. Turn left on 642, which goes downhill, crosses the Laurel Fork, and climbs Middle Mountain. At the top of the mountain, the road turns sharply right. On the left is a dirt road and a sign pointing left toward the Middle Mountain Trail. Drive up the dirt road—not the private driveway to the left of it—for 1.1 km (0.7 mi.) and park in the small parking area.
Trail description: The Middle Mountain Trail begins at the gate to the meadow on the west. You will be walking on private land for 0.5 km (0.3 mi.) until you pass another gate. Please respect your access privilege!

One hundred meters beyond this gate, turn sharply right onto a somewhat washed-out dirt road, which goes uphill in a sweeping curve across an open field or meadow. After 200 m on this road and immediately beside it, there is a large rounded rock pile, 3 m high and 6 m wide at its base. A hundred meters beyond this rock pile are a fence, a gate, and a Forest Service sign. Behind this gate the trail continues on public land.

Follow the old jeep road into the woods. The trail then goes downhill, passing a road going off to the left (west). Here you will find a large stand of hemlocks.

The trail now generally follows the ridgeline, with ups and downs of less than one hundred meters. There are several logging roads on the left (west). Ignore them.

At 2.7 km (1.7 mi.) from the car, in an open area at the bottom of a downhill stretch, you will reach a fork where the Christian Run Trail drops off to the west. This junction makes a good campsite, but the nearest water is 1.3 km (0.8 mi.) away, down Christian Run Trail.

Past this junction, the Middle Mountain Trail narrows at a log gate and becomes strictly a footpath. It follows the ridge top uphill for 0.8 km (0.5 mi.) to a level area and a Y in the trail. The left branch of the Y peters out in a little while.

Taking the right branch of the Y down the east side of the ridge, you will look northwest into the drainage of Cold Spring. Here you will have to make a choice: Either return the way you came, or bushwhack down from the ridge via Cold Spring Run to the Laurel Fork.

Cold Spring Run:

This is not a trail, so follow directions carefully and, if possible, use a topographic map and compass.

Leave Middle Mountain Trail 0.8 km (0.5 mi.) past the Y at the point where the trail turns sharply right, and angle down the slope, going north. About 0.3 km (0.2 mi.) below is the source of Cold Spring Run.

Find the creek and follow it downstream to the Laurel Fork. It is 1.9 km (1.2 mi.) from where you left the Middle Mountain Trail to the Laurel Fork, and the bushwhacking is fairly easy.

At the bottom you should arrive at the Laurel Fork Trail, which will take you south up the Laurel Fork to Buck Run and the other trail junctions. It is 1.1 km (0.7 mi.) from Cold Spring Run to Buck Run. You will have to wade, crossing the Laurel Fork opposite Buck Run.

CHRISTIAN RUN TRAIL

Length: 2.6 kilometers (1.6 miles)
Direction of travel: Northwest
Difficulty: Easy
Elevation: 1,144–900 meters (3,750–2,950 feet)
Difference in elevation: 244 meters (800 feet)
Markings: Intermittent blue blazes
Trail #: 599
How to get there: The Christian Run Trail starts 2.7 km (1.7 mi.) from the beginning of the Middle Mountain Trail. The opposite end of the trail can be reached by following the Laurel Fork Trail.
Trail description: The trail, a grassy track, starts at a beautiful meadow on the west slope of Middle Mountain. You will probably lose the trail in the summer in the high grass. Pick it up again farther downhill, where the trail entering the woods becomes evident.

After a very short time, if it is summer, you may encounter waist-high nettles, so you should be wearing long pants and a shirt or sweater for protection. You can lift your arms above the sea of nettles.

As you proceed downhill, the nettles eventually disappear. When they no longer hold your attention, you will notice you are entering a beautiful stand of hemlocks. Christian Run bubbles on your left at some distance from the trail.

Follow the trail downstream to the Laurel Fork. A trail marker indicates the junction with the Laurel Fork Trail.

3
Ramsey's Draft Wilderness

The Ramsey's Draft area is located in Augusta and Highland counties. The land bordering Ramsey's Draft—a clear trout stream—was one of the first tracts to be acquired by the U.S. Forest Service when George Washington National Forest was established. No settlers ever lived in the steep, narrow valley, for they would have been unable to carve out a living. There is practically no flat terrain along Ramsey's Draft that would lend itself to building a house and a garden, let alone farming. But the remains of a pioneer settlement, including an old cemetery, can be found at Puffenbarger Pond, near where Forest Development Road 95 crosses Shenandoah Mountain. Some inscriptions on the stones marking the graves can still be deciphered.

The parallel ridges of Shenandoah Mountain on the west and Bald Ridge on the east plus a connecting ridge form a roughly horseshoe-shaped mountain; the terrain within the horseshoe is drained by Ramsey's Draft. The exterior slope of the horseshoe lies in several other watersheds, namely Shaw Fork on the west, the Calfpasture River on the east, and the North River on the north.

The distance between Shenandoah Mountain and Bald Ridge is about 4 kilometers (2.5 miles) as the crow flies. These ridges rise approximately 300 meters (1,000 feet) above the valley floor. The terrain is characterized by steep slopes almost everywhere except near the eastern perimeter.

There are pockets of virgin forest in Ramsey's Draft—a rarity in the central Appalachians. Perhaps as much as 24.3 square kilometers (6,000 acres) have never been subjected to the axe and chain saw. The huge hemlocks, white pines, oaks, and yellow poplars are in remarkable contrast to smaller trees found nearby.

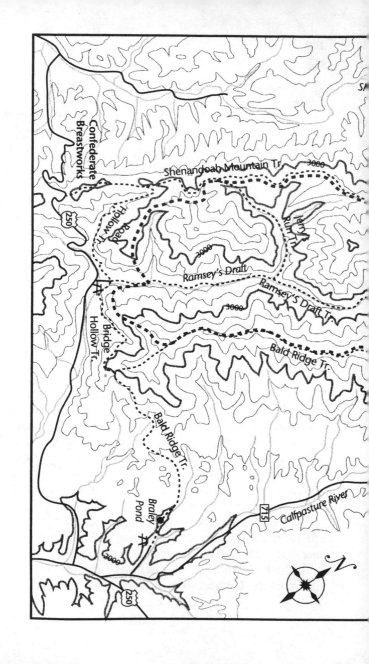

You can experience a sensation of true wilderness in the hemlock forest along the upper prongs of Ramsey's Draft, where there is a deeply shaded understory of moss and ferns. In other places the forest has different aspects. On some mountain ridges the forest floor is carpeted with grass, and in some steep ravines large trees grow directly out of stony slopes that seem almost devoid of soil cover. Azaleas and mountain laurel are common. Small wildflowers are abundant, especially before trees come into full foliage in the spring.

Hunters in great numbers are attracted during hunting season. If you plan a hike at that time, wear some blaze orange (no light colors though) and be noisy—talk, sing, or whistle so there will be no mistake about your species identity. Or stay home altogether.

Ravens and pileated woodpeckers are among the more noticeable birds. Breeding birds include several northern species, such as the winter wren and the Canada and blackburnian warblers, that find suitable habitats in the dense virgin hemlock forests.

An area measuring 27.1 square kilometers (6,700 acres) within Ramsey's Draft was designated a wilderness by Congress. Although it protects the horseshoe-shaped valley and the virgin forests, this area includes only the interior sides of the valley up to the ridge top of the surrounding mountains.

On the eastern side of Bald Ridge there are a number of old jeep trails, which start from Augusta County Road 715. Many just peter out once they reach the steeper slopes of the mountain, generally at an elevation of around 760 meters (2,500 feet). One road, however, leads to the picnic area at Braley Pond, which is an artificial impoundment. This road, paved at its beginning, leaves Augusta County Road 715 about 0.6 km (0.4 mi.) north of U.S. 250. From the picnic area, a trail on the right side of the pond will guide you to the start of the Bald Ridge Trail.

Camping spots are numerous along the outer perimeter of the Ramsey's Draft area, especially along Forest Development roads 95 and 96. The water of the North River constitutes part of the water supply for Staunton. The riverbanks have been protected against erosion by gabions—medium-sized stones piled high and held in place by wire mesh.

There is a picnic area beside U.S. 250 at the beginning of the Ramsey's Draft Trail, but camping is not permitted there. There are many good camping spots along this trail though. Whenever possible, try to use the established campsites, with their fire rings, rather than building new ones.

Ramsey's Draft Trail has many fords. A few can be crossed dry-footed, but for others wading is the only choice, so plan on wet feet.

A number of circular hikes are possible. For example, if you park at the picnic area, you could hike up Ramsey's Draft Trail to Jerry's Run Trail and up to the Shenandoah Mountain Trail, which you would then hike toward the Confederate Breastworks and down the Road Hollow Trail back to the picnic area. Or, if you do not mind walking along a forest development road for a bit, there are other possibilities on the eastern side of the area. Check the map and make up your own hike.

All trails in Ramsey's Draft are maintained at a minimum level consistent with its wilderness status. That includes to a large extent the blazes for the trails; they exist outside the wilderness boundary but may stop completely once you're inside. The Forest Service does put up trail signs, but, of course, these are subject to vandalism by both bears and humans.

Maps: USGS West Augusta, Palo Alto, and McDowell quadrangles, 7.5 minute series; Ramsey's Draft Wilderness map, George Washington National Forest.

SHENANDOAH MOUNTAIN TRAIL

Length: 17.2 kilometers (10.7 miles)
Direction of travel: Generally north
Difficulty: Moderate
Elevation: 890–1,244–915 meters (2,920–4,080– 3,000 feet)
Difference in elevation: 354–329 meters (1,160–1,080 feet)

Markings: Blue blazes (outside the wilderness area)
Trail #: 447
How to get there: The trailhead is at a scenic turnout on U.S. 250 just as it crosses the crest of Shenandoah Mountain, 26.9 km (16.7 mi.) west of Churchville. Approached from the west, the turnout is 29 km (18 mi.) from Monterey on U.S. 250. Park at the turnout. The turnout is marked CONFEDERATE BREASTWORKS.

This is a one-way trail, so you will need a car shuttle at the end. To get to the termination of the trail if you are coming from Churchville, turn off U.S. 250 to the right immediately after passing the bridge over the Calfpasture River. You will then be on County Road 715. (Coming from Monterey, the turnoff is just before the bridge and to the left.) The pavement of 715 ends at 5.3 km (3.3 mi.), and the road becomes Forest Development Road 96. At 10 km (6.2 mi.) FDR 96 joins FDR 95. Turn left onto FDR 95. At 21.7 km (13.5 mi.), 250 m (550 ft.) after you pass FDR 85 entering from the north, the Shenandoah Mountain trailhead is on the left. A small opening in the woods marks the trail's beginning.

Trail description: The trail starts on the northwest side of the turnout on U.S. 250. After entering the trail beyond the retaining wall at the parking lot, turn right to follow the trail (straight ahead is a somewhat washed-out gully from the top of the hill—this is *not* the trail). After a few meters you will come to a junction: On the left is a shorter trail going steeply up the hill; straight ahead lies a longer, more gentle ascent. These two trails actually form the circuit hike of the Confederate Breastworks—a walk of about thirty to forty-five minutes. The actual Shenandoah Mountain Trail starts where these two trails meet again, just behind the top of the hill, and follows the side of the mountain to the left (west). The walking becomes easy at this point.

At 2.4 km (1.5 mi.) from U.S. 250 you will come to the junction with the new Road Hollow Trail, which in 4 km (2.5 mi.) will take you to the Mountain House Picnic Area.

The trail continues winding its way through open woods along the ridge of Shenandoah Mountain, with only very minor ups and

downs. At times you will find nice views, especially during the winter months, after the leaves have fallen.

Just before the junction with Jerry's Run Trail at 4.3 km (2.7 mi.), you will enter the wilderness area, marked with a sign and trail register. Jerry's Run Trail branches off to the right. Down the trail, the former site of Sexton Cabin is 0.7 km (0.4 mi.) distant, and Ramsey's Draft Trail 3.2 km (2 mi.). A trail on the left to Shaw Fork has practically vanished due to lack of use. The land along Shaw Fork is privately owned, and you should not trespass.

The Shenandoah Mountain Trail continues level near the ridge of Shenandoah Mountain for slightly more than 8 km (5 mi.), through woods. On the east side of the ridge it passes through an open forest of sometimes very large hardwoods, whereas on the more steeply sloping west side of the ridge it leads through scrubby oaks and pines, with an understory of mountain laurel. At 11.6 km (7.2 mi.) you will meet a fork in the trail: Stay to the right. Before long the trail passes through a grassy clearing, where you will find a wilderness boundary sign. From this clearing the Sinclair Hollow Trail leaves to the left and descends the west side of the mountain. The first 100 m are very faint. The Shenandoah Mountain Trail continues straight ahead past the clearing.

At 12.6 km (7.8 mi.) you will arrive at the upper end of Ramsey's Draft Trail. It runs into the Shenandoah Mountain Trail from the right (east) in a small saddle with an open forest of very large trees. Six smallish evergreens, about 1 m apart in a straight line, make a good landmark at this point. A spring, which is dry in late summer, can be found a few meters down the west slope of the mountain, opposite Ramsey's Draft Trail.

The Shenandoah Mountain Trail now passes along the west slope of several knobs, and at 15.4 km (9.6 mi.) from the trailhead the path begins to drop downhill at a moderate rate. There are some excellent views here looking northwest into West Virginia's Pendelton County.

Continue hiking downhill. At 16.6 km (10.3 mi.) you will reach a small grassy meadow. On the west side of this clearing is a narrow, unmarked deer trail that leads sharply downhill toward Puffenbarger Pond. It soon vanishes completely, but by following the ridge downhill through the woods one eventually encounters the old meadows and apple trees that remain from early settlers in this area. This route is for the adventurous only!

The Shenandoah Mountain Trail leaves the meadow on the opposite side, bears sharply east, and then continues downhill. Following it, you will cross a small creek at 17.2 km (10.7 mi.) and arrive at FDR 95.

RAMSEY'S DRAFT TRAIL

Length: 11.3 kilometers (7 miles)
Direction of travel: Generally north and west
Difficulty: At first level and easy, except in flood-affected regions; later steep and more strenuous
Elevation: 687–1,232 meters (2,252–4,040 feet)
Difference in elevation: 545 meters (1,788 feet)
Markings: None, but trail mostly easy to follow
Trail #: 440
How to get there: Drive west on U.S. 250 from Churchville to the Mountain House Picnic Area, on the right at 23.5 km (14.6 mi.). From the picnic area, take the road across a small concrete bridge to the rear parking area. Ramsey's Draft Trail starts as a continuation of the entrance road, beyond the parking area. The other end of the trail can be reached via the Shenandoah Mountain Trail.
Trail description: In 1985, a week of heavy rains caused a flood that tore out large sections of Ramsey's Draft Trail, which previously had been an easy-to-follow woods road. Now only bits and pieces of the road are left, and at times you will be on your own to find your way across or along the side of the stream. You cannot get lost because the steep mountains on either side of Ramsey's Draft will keep you on course.

From the parking area follow the Ramsey's Draft Trail straight ahead along the left side of the stream. A side trail to the right leads across a foot bridge, which consists of a flattened log with a handrail. Shortly thereafter, the Bridge Hollow Trail leaves to the left.

There are many logjams and parts of washed-out concrete from the fords of the old road. You can usually find your way over and around them by following footpaths of varying distinctness, unless another flood just washed them out. Then you are on your own.

The difficulty of the stream crossings will vary greatly with the seasons: In late summer Ramsey's Draft flows mostly under the gravel left by the flood, and it appears dry except where the water flows over exposed bedrock. In the spring, the water may be sufficiently deep, cold, and fast-moving to make the crossings difficult and uncomfortable.

The narrow valley is densely wooded and some magnificent large trees can be found. In many places the forest floor beneath these trees is deeply shaded and free of undergrowth. Here you can find many fine campsites with established fire rings.

At 3.4 km (2.1 mi.) Jerry's Run joins Ramsey's Draft, just at the end of an especially long and severe flood washout of the woods road. Shortly afterward Jerry's Run Trail branches off to the west from Ramsey's Draft Trail.

Ramsey's Draft Trail continues with intermittent sections of the woods road and several long stretches with obstructions resulting from the flood.

At 6.6 km (4.1 mi.) Ramsey's Draft branches into a left prong and a right prong. Up to this point part of the trail was an old road, but it becomes a foot trail here and follows the right prong.

A trail sign and a USGS benchmark giving the elevation as 889 m (2,914 ft.) are located on the west side of the trail, at the end of the old road section.

Ramsey's Draft Trail now begins to climb noticeably. You are traveling through an area with very large hemlocks. This is virgin timber—a rarity in Virginia. The hemlock forest continues far up the trail, though not to the ridgeline. There are few campsites along this section of the trail because of the steepness of the terrain.

The trail now climbs through open woods with large trees. At 8.1 km (5 mi.) the trail turns 90 degrees to the west. Near this bend, you will cross an underground stream coming from the east. With some careful searching you may find a few rocky campsites here in a beautiful setting. Ahead are small mossy waterfalls along Ramsey's Draft.

You may occasionally encounter a large tree that has fallen across the path, unless a trail crew has been through recently. Climb over these obstructions rather than going around them. The latter practice often causes erosion.

At 9.5 km (5.9 mi.) is the junction with Tearjacket Trail, coming in from the northeast. Lots of skunk cabbage grow here in the summer.

About 200 m (656 ft.) below this trail junction, cross Ramsey's Draft for the last time. The stream here is very small, but it is the last water you can count on finding. A hundred meters west of the trail junction is a campsite near the spring that is the source of the right prong of Ramsey's Draft, which may be dry in late summer.

Continuing west along the Ramsey's Draft Trail from this junction, after an additional 0.6 km (0.4 mi.), you will come to the beginning of the Hardscrabble Knob Trail (10.1 km; 6.3 mi. from the start of the trail). From here Ramsey's Draft Trail descends slightly toward its junction with the Shenandoah Mountain Trail at 11.3 km (7 mi.).

You have now left the large trees far behind you. The hike here leads through younger woods with some undergrowth, including beautiful azaleas and many suckers of the American chestnut, which grow 3 to 7 m (10 to 20 ft.) tall from the old rootstocks before being attacked by the blight.

You will arrive at the Shenandoah Mountain Trail in a clear wooded area with many large trees (11.3 km; 7 mi.). The junction is marked by a row of six spruce trees planted fairly close together and also by signs. There is a spring near the junction of Shenandoah Mountain and Ramsey's Draft trails, a few meters down the west slope of the mountain.

HARDSCRABBLE KNOB TRAIL

Length: 0.6 kilometer (0.4 mile)
Direction of travel: South
Difficulty: Easy
Elevation: 1,232–1,306 meters (4,040–4,282 feet)
Difference in elevation: 74 meters (242 feet)
Markings: None
Trail #: 440A
How to get there: The trail begins at 9.3 km (5.8 mi.) up the Ramsey's Draft Trail. The trailhead can also be reached by hiking 1.1 km (0.7 mi.) down the Ramsey's Draft Trail from its terminus at the Shenandoah Mountain Trail.

Trail description: There is a much-used campsite—no water—at the trailhead, and a sign pointing to Hardscrabble Knob. You may find water at a spring several hundred meters east of the trailhead, along the Ramsey's Draft Trail, but this supply is dependable only from late fall through spring.

Hardscrabble Knob Trail climbs slightly but steadily to the south toward Hardscrabble Knob, at an elevation of 1,306 m (4,282 ft.). The knob is the highest point along Ramsey's Draft.

In summer, the trail may be heavily overgrown with fern and other plants. At 0.6 km (0.4 mi.) you will reach an abandoned cabin on the left side of the trail near the knob. There are several campsites here, although no water is available.

Hardscrabble Knob Trail continues for 50 m past the cabin to the rock outcrop, which is Hardscrabble Knob. Views are obscured by trees in the summer and aren't exactly stupendous in winter, either.

JERRY'S RUN TRAIL

Length: 3.2 kilometers (2 miles)
Direction of travel: West
Difficulty: Moderate

Elevation: 769–964 meters (2,520–3,160 feet)
Difference in elevation: 195 meters (640 feet)
Markings: None, but trail obvious
Trail #: 441
How to get there: The trail begins 3.4 km (2.1 mi.) up the Ramsey's Draft Trail. The opposite end can be reached via the Shenandoah Mountain Trail.
Trail description: The trail climbs steadily to the west and toward the Shenandoah Mountain Trail 3.2 km (2 mi.) away.

The trail crosses Jerry's Run several times but, except during very high water, most crossings can be made on rocks or by jumping. For the first 0.8 km (0.5 mi.), there are several established campsites ready for use and complete with fire rings.

At 2.6 km (1.6 mi.) you will enter a grassy open area at the former site of Sexton Cabin. The concrete foundation and the fireplace are all that remain of the cabin.

Jerry's Run Trail crosses the stream just below the cabin site and climbs steadily until it reaches the crest of Shenandoah Mountain and the Shenandoah Mountain Trail at 3.2 km (2 mi.)

By the latter trail, the junction with the northern end of the Ramsey's Draft Trail is 8.2 km (5.1 mi.) and with Forest Development Road 95, 12.9 km (8 mi.) to the north. The new Road Hollow Trail is 1.9 km (1.2 mi.) and U.S. 250 is 4.3 km (2.7 mi.) distant to the south.

WILD OAK TRAIL

Length: 8.4 kilometers (5.2 miles)
Direction of travel: West and north
Difficulty: Moderate to strenuous
Elevation: 705–1,256 meters (2,312–4,120 feet)
Difference in elevation: 551 meters (1,808 feet)
Markings: White plastic diamonds
Trail #: 716

The Wild Oak Trail forms a 41.2 km (25.6 mi.) loop, only part of which lies within the Ramsey's Draft area. Most sections were formerly called by different names, which still appear on many maps. The sections described here were previously called the Dividing Ridge and Springhouse Ridge trails.

How to get there: Approaching from Churchville, turn off U.S. 250 to the right onto County Road 715 immediately after passing the bridge over the Calfpasture River. Approached from the west, the turnoff is just before the bridge and to the left. After the pavement ends at 5.3 km (3.3 mi.), the road becomes Forest Development Road 96. You will reach the trailhead, where FDR 96 crosses the height-of-land, 6.8 km (4.2 mi.) after leaving U.S. 250. There is a small parking space for three or four cars on the left.

The opposite end of this trail can be reached by continuing along FDR 96 to the junction with FDR 95. Turn left on 95. You will reach Camp Todd, with numerous undeveloped campsites, 14.8 km (9.2 mi.) from U.S. 250. Walk along the trail at the sign describing the camp's history. About 20 m south of a water pump—before you reach it—the trail starts to the left across a small ravine.

Trail description: A berm blocks vehicle access to the trail to the west. At first the walking is rather level. About 500 m from the parking lot the trail divides. The Wild Oak Trail is straight ahead; an old woods road wanders off to the right along the hillside and then down again.

Follow the Wild Oak Trail, with its occasional white plastic diamonds. Soon, the trail starts climbing very steeply along the crest of Dividing Ridge, with loose rocks and dirt making the footing treacherous at times.

At 3.4 km (2.1 mi.) you will reach a saddle, where there usually is a small stagnant pond with no inflow or outflow. The water *cannot* be drunk even after treatment. This section is grassy and full of mosquitoes and flies in the summer. There are a few limited views. The Bald Ridge Trail starts to the south near the pond, following along the crest of Bald Ridge and eventually descending to the picnic area at Braley Pond (11.1 km; 6.9 mi.).

The Wild Oak Trail climbs steeply from the other side of the pond, then levels, turning north.

About 25 m after the summit of Big Bald Knob, which is a grassy clearing with no view, you will come to a short new path on your right leading to the edge of the ridge and a beautiful view over the valley. After this side path, the main trail descends to the junction with Tearjacket Trail at 6 km (3.7 mi.). There is a wilderness registry box at the intersection. To the west, Ramsey's Draft Trail is 1.9 km (1.2 mi.) down the Tearjacket Trail. (The closest water is a spring on the Ramsey's Draft Trail near that junction.) Hardscrabble Knob Trail (via the Ramsey's Draft Trail) is 2.6 km (1.6 mi.) away.

Turn right to continue on the Springhouse Ridge section of the Wild Oak Trail. At first the walking is almost level, then the trail descends more steeply with several switchbacks, reaching Camp Todd at 8.4 km (5.2 mi.). About 300 m before the trail reaches Camp Todd, a creekbed, usually dry, lies below to the right (south).

TEARJACKET TRAIL

Length: 1.9 kilometers (1.2 miles)
Direction of travel: Generally west
Difficulty: Easy
Elevation: 1,113–1,195 meters (3,650–3,920 feet)
Difference in elevation: 82 meters (270 feet)
Markings: None, but trail easy to follow
Trail #: 426
How to get there: The Tearjacket Trail begins 2.4 km (1.5 mi.) from Camp Todd on Wild Oak Trail. The other end can be reached via Ramsey's Draft Trail 1.8 km (1.1 mi.) from its junction with the Shenandoah Mountain Trail.
Trail description: Starting at the Wild Oak Trail, the Tearjacket Trail leads through open woods, first descending very slightly and

then climbing gently to its junction with Ramsey's Draft Trail. There are no views along the way.

The trail does not lead over Tearjacket Knob, nor does any side trail that we could find. And in our experience so far, Tearjacket Trail has not lived up to its descriptive name.

At the junction of Tearjacket and Ramsey's Draft trails, you will find a nice campsite with a spring close by.

From this point Hardscrabble Knob Trail begins 0.6 km (0.4 mi.) to the west; Shenandoah Mountain Trail is 1.8 km (1.1 mi.) west, and FDR 95, via Shenandoah Mountain Trail, is 6.4 km (4 mi.) distant. To the east and south, via Ramsey's Draft Trail, it is 6.1 km (3.8 mi.) to the beginning of Jerry's Run Trail and 9.5 km (5.9 mi.) to the parking facilities near U.S. 250.

BALD RIDGE TRAIL

Length: 11.1 kilometers (6.9 miles)
Direction of travel: Generally north
Difficulty: Difficult
Elevation: 880–1,170 meters (2,000–3,900 feet)
Difference in elevation: 830 meters (1,900 feet)
Markings: Intermittent yellow plastic diamonds
Trail #: 496
How to get there: Approaching from Churchville via U.S. 250, turn right onto County Road 715 immediately after crossing the Calfpasture River. After 0.6 km (0.4 mi.), turn left to the Braley Pond Picnic Area, where parking is available. Follow the trail around the right side of Braley Pond and cross a footbridge over the stream that feeds the pond. Immediately after crossing the footbridge, turn right onto a woods road. This is the start of the Bald Ridge Trail.

The other end of the trail can be reached via the Wild Oak Trail.
Trail description: The Bald Ridge Trail shows signs of recent maintenance work in some places, but in other areas it has faded to invisibility. Even where it has completely vanished, however, its

general route along the ridge can usually be followed without much difficulty. Carrying a topographic map and compass will help keep you headed in the right direction at a few points where side ridges branch off to the east or west.

From its starting point just above Braley Pond, the trail ascends very gently as a woods road and passes through three grassy game clearings within the first 0.8 km (0.5 mi.). Beyond the third clearing the trail crosses a small stream, and after another 50 m it turns right off the woods road. A sign marks this point, and two log steps are set into the bank of the road.

From here the trail follows on or near a ridge for about 0.8 km (0.5 mi.) and then climbs at a steady rate along the hillside. In some places along this ascent there are excellent views of the mountains and valleys to the south through the open woods.

At several points, especially just after crossing ravines, the trail traverses regions of rather soft soil on a steep hillside and is badly eroded and very faint. It is usually easy to pick up again as it enters more solid ground. As you approach the top of the ridge, however, you will encounter a longer section of vanished trail. Ribbons or other markers may or may not be present to mark the route. If lost, you can simply continue up the hillside until you gain the crest. The trail itself reaches the ridge top at 4.6 km (2.9 mi.), shortly after its junction with the Bridge Hollow Trail.

From this point on, the trail follows the crest to the north or northeast, going over or around several small knobs or peaks. The highest points, rising at most 100 m above the ridgeline, are called The Peak, The Pinnacle, and Gordon's Peak—none with a view. The trail has been maintained principally by occasional usage, so that it is clear and well worn where its course is obvious (such as along the top of narrow ridges) but becomes obscure or vanishes altogether in places where the best route is ambiguous.

For the first kilometer after reaching the top of Bald Ridge, it is easiest to bypass the peaks on the right (east) side. The last and largest of these is The Peak, the summit of which is an uninspiring tangle of dense brush.

After passing The Peak, continue to the north along Bald Ridge, climbing over the tops of subsequent knobs and sometimes bypassing them on the left (west) side. The trail is faint in many places but not necessary anyway. The open forest that grows along the ridgetop makes walking without a trail easy and, in fact, delightful. The wilderness feeling experienced along this seldom-traveled ridge is as fine as any you can obtain within the Ramsey's Draft Wilderness.

After Gordon's Peak the trail, here fortunately well maintained, passes through a thicket of mountain laurel and finally ends at a small stagnant pond and the junction with Wild Oak Trail. To the right (east) it is 3.4 km (2.1 mi.) to FDR 96. To the left you can follow Wild Oak Trail to the junction with Tearjacket Trail (2.6 km; 1.6 mi.) and down to Camp Todd and FDR 95 (2.4 km; 1.5 mi.). It is 1.9 km (1.2 mi.) along Tearjacket Trail to Ramsey's Draft Trail.

SINCLAIR HOLLOW TRAIL

Length: 2.9 kilometers (1.8 miles)
Direction of travel: Southeast
Difficulty: Moderate
Elevation: 760–990 meters (2,500–3,250 feet)
Difference in elevation: 230 meters (750 feet)
Markings: None
Trail #: 447D
How to get there: Approaching from Churchville, turn off U.S. 250 to the right onto County Road 715 immediately after passing the bridge over the Calfpasture River. Approached from the west, the turnoff is just before the bridge and to the left. The pavement ends at 5.3 km (3.3 mi.), and the road becomes Forest Development Road 96. At the junction with FDR 95 turn left. After about 12.1 km (7.5 mi.) the road will fork (keep right) and start to descend steeply. After 1.6 km (1 mi.) down the hill, turn left on FDR 64. After snaking along the hillside for 9.8 km (6 mi.), you come to a gate,

which is open only from mid-October to January 1. It is 0.8 km (0.5 mi.) to the start of the Sinclair Hollow Trail on the left. The trail is marked only by a sign depicting a hiking figure.

The other end of the trail can be reached via the Shenandoah Mountain Trail.

Trail description: The Sinclair Hollow Trail starts on the left as an old logging road. The trail first crosses a streambed, then two "tank traps" to keep out ATVs.

About 0.5 km (0.3 mi.) later, you will pass a game pond on the left. At 1.2 km (0.7 mi.) you come to a small grassy clearing.

The woods are at first mostly hemlocks and pines, with hardwoods interspersed. Later the forest is mostly deciduous.

During the first half of the hike you will cross the creek twice more. After that there is no other source of water along the trail.

At 1.6 km (1 mi.) the old logging road becomes a foot trail and begins to ascend steeply up the side of a ridge. Near the top the climb becomes more moderate until you gain the crest of Shenandoah Mountain.

The Sinclair Hollow Trail meets the Shenandoah Mountain Trail in a grassy clearing in a saddle. No sign marks the junction; only a small metal sign proclaims the wilderness boundary.

BRIDGE HOLLOW TRAIL

Length: 3.2 kilometers (2 miles)
Direction of travel: Generally southeast
Difficulty: Moderate
Elevation: 689–1,012 meters (2,260–3,320 feet)
Difference in elevation: 323 meters (1,060 feet)
Markings: Occasional yellow diamonds
Trail #: 442
How to get there: Via the Ramsey's Draft Trail. The opposite end can be reached via the Bald Ridge Trail.
Trail description: From the parking area follow the Ramsey's Draft

Trail over the footbridge—a flattened log with a handrail—across Ramsey's Draft.

Follow the trail through a grove of hemlocks for about 20 m to the side of the mountain. Here the trail begins its ascent toward Bald Ridge. This is a narrow foot trail clinging to the side of the mountain; be careful of your footing—if you step closely to the outside edge of the trail, your foot may slip, thereby wearing away the trail.

At first the trail climbs steeply off the valley floor, but it soon levels off to a more gradual but steady climb.

The trail switches back on itself several times in narrow ravines and crosses two rock slides, but it is well built up in these areas.

Nettles grow in wet spots on the trail; in late May they are about knee-high. You may consider wearing long pants later in summer.

The trail passes mostly through open woods. There are a couple of places with many large mountain laurels, which, when in bloom in late spring, make for a beautiful hike.

At 3.2 km (2.0 mi.) the trail reaches its junction with the Bald Ridge Trail, close to the first knob on the ridge. The spot is marked with several yellow diamond markers and, nailed to a tree, a wooden sign pointing left to Bald Ridge and its eventual junction with the Wild Oak Trail. A right turn will lead you downhill to Braley Pond.

ROAD HOLLOW TRAIL

Length: 4 kilometers (2.5 miles)
Direction of travel: Northwest
Difficulty: Moderate
Elevation: 689–914 meters (2,260–3,000 feet)
Difference in elevation: 225 meters (740 feet)
Markings: None
Trail #: 448
How to get there: Via the Ramsey's Draft and the Shenandoah Mountain trails. Signs are posted at both ends of the trail.

Trail description: About 150 m from the parking area at the start of the Ramsey's Draft Trail, you will come to the junction with the Road Hollow Trail on the left.

This trail was built to allow hikers access from the top of Shenandoah Mountain to Ramsey's Draft without having to walk along U.S. 250 and thereby be exposed to the traffic.

The Road Hollow Trail hugs the hillside in Road Hollow between 30 m and 50 m above the stream. It was dug into the slope on the right side of the hollow. The stream is dry during most of the year, although you might find some water in spring.

The ascent is moderate but steady. The trail leads through mixed hardwoods all the way to the top of Shenandoah Mountain, with no scenic views anywhere. On the lower parts of the trail you can hear the traffic from U.S. 250, but later an intervening ridge screens out the noise.

After 4 km (2.5 mi.) you will reach the junction with the Shenandoah Mountain Trail. To the right are the junctions with Jerry's Run (1.6 km; 1 mi.) and Ramsey's Draft trails, to the left are the Confederate Breastworks and U.S. 250 (2.4 km; 1.5 mi.).

4
Crawford Mountain Area

Crawford Mountain is part of Augusta County's Great North Mountain, which forms the western boundary of the Shenandoah valley and the first ridges of the Alleghenies.

Crawford Mountain itself apparently has always been woodland with few, if any, pioneer settlers. There is evidence, however, of early clearing over an extensive tract on the higher slopes of McKittrick's Ridge, perhaps for grazing. The remainder of the mountain has been logged over at least once on a commercial scale before its acquisition by the U.S. Forest Service in 1921. Since then, the mountain has been largely left alone. Management is under the multiple-use designation, but timbering so far has been limited to two or three relatively small tracts, all at the periphery. Game management likewise has remained minimal, with two small clearings and no road access. A corridor for a Virginia Electric and Power Company power line cuts across the northwestern corner.

In all, the tract is remarkably wild and unspoiled. Crawford Mountain is a very rewarding place for a hike: The trails are all closed to motorized traffic, the woods are deep, and the solitude is impressive.

Crawford Mountain consists of a ridge and its outliers and considerable lower land. The lowlands are broken terrain with many small ravines, hillocks, and streambeds. The mountain proper tends to be on the dry side, with few active streams. Quite a few of the creeks shown on maps dry up in late summer.

Trees cover the entire mountain. They are mostly medium-sized hardwoods, with a few large specimens. There is little understory, giving a feeling of openness to the woods. You can find occasional large white pines and hemlocks along streams at lower elevations,

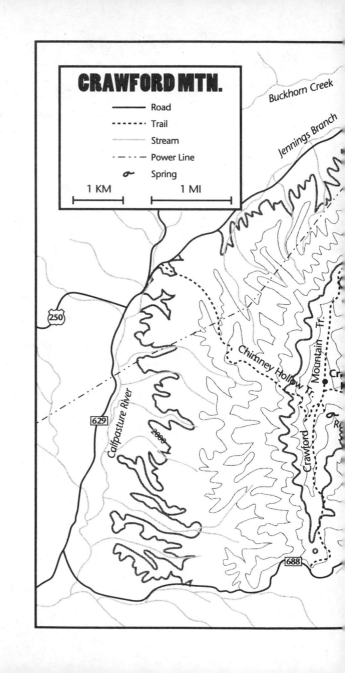

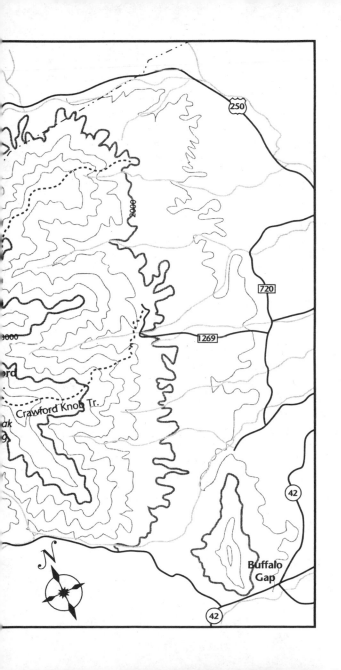

where some rhododendron also grow. There is probably no virgin forest on Crawford Mountain, although the aspect is certainly one of maturity. The best views can be seen during winter, after leaves have fallen, but a few unobstructed views may be had at any time from vantage points along the Crawford Mountain Trail.

In the spring, before the leaves come out, a wide variety of wildflowers, including dwarf iris, grow in the woods.

Especially for rock hounds: Some fossils, such as brachiopods, may be found in rocky streambeds and nearby cliffs or outcrops, particularly near County Road 688 west of the height-of-land between Crawford Mountain and Elliott Knob.

The climate of the region is generally mild, but in winter it is colder and snowier than in nearby Shenandoah valley. Travelers in this season should be prepared for severe weather. The average winter temperature is 0 degrees Celsius (32 degrees Fahrenheit).

No camping or fire permits are necessary. The mountain is dry, and there is only one spring located close enough to trails to be useful (see map and Crawford Mountain Trail description).

There are no private inholdings on Crawford Mountain. Some private land exists on the periphery of the tract.

There has been considerable abuse by and illegal use of ATVs on the Crawford Mountain Trail, resulting in erosion and double treads on the trails. The Forest Service may have to reroute the trail if damage becomes too severe.

In the Deerfield Ranger District, foot trails are marked by a yellow plastic diamond.

Maps: USGS Churchville, Elliott Knob, Stokesville, and West Augusta quadrangles, 7.5 minute series; Deerfield Ranger District map, George Washington National Forest.

CRAWFORD KNOB TRAIL

Length: 9.1 kilometers (5.7 miles)
Direction of travel: West
Difficulty: Moderate

Elevation: 554–1,137 meters (1,816–3,728 feet)
Difference in elevation: 583 meters (1,912 feet)
Markings: Yellow plastic diamonds
Trail #: 487
How to get there: Go 16.9 km (10.5 mi.) west from Staunton on U.S. 250 to the village of Lone Fountain. Turn left on County Road 720, and proceed 3.7 km (2.3 mi.) to a gravel road on the right immediately past Jerusalem Church, Forest Development Road 1269. Park your car so that you do not block the gate, which is probably open only during the hunting season.

The opposite end of the trail can be reached via the Crawford Mountain Trail.

Trail description: Follow FDR 1269, which is a public right-of-way leading through posted private land, for approximately 3.2 km (2 mi.) until you see the sign for the Crawford Knob Trail on the left. The road ends in a rather large turnaround about 200 m later.

The trail threads its way along the hillside, ascending steadily through deciduous woods. On your left, you may glimpse the road you came up through the trees.

Having moved away from the private land, the trail begins to descend towards a creek, McKittricks Branch. You will find more pines here than earlier. The creek may be dry in August, but as its bed is fairly wide, you may not have much trouble crossing it dry footed, even in the wet season. The scramble up the bank on the other side is something else, though—it is extremely steep and slippery.

Upon reaching the top of the bank, you will find yourself on an old woods road. Turn right here. Watch carefully for the yellow plastic diamonds. After a few meters the trail turns off to the left. Unfortunately there are no double diamonds to alert you to the turn.

(If you follow the old woods road uphill you will come to two small grassy clearings. Upon reaching the second clearing, step to the right through the trees to the banks of the creek, and you will find some pretty step falls. The woods road ends at this clearing.)

Back where the Crawford Mountain Trail turns off the woods

road, the trail almost immediately starts a steep climb up the mountainside. There are a number of switchbacks—some of them either poorly constructed or else eroded by hikers.

The forest scenery changes from large trees to a more scrubby look. As the trail gains altitude, mountain laurel makes its appearance. Depending upon how recently the trail has been maintained, you may find it clear or overgrown and hard to follow. There are some good views back over the Shenandoah valley and, later, views southwest toward the southern main ridge of Crawford Mountain.

You will reach the wooded summit of Crawford Knob at 8 km (5 mi.). The knob is an outlier of the main Crawford Mountain ridge. You are 1,137 m (3,728 ft.) above sea level here.

The trail now descends slightly. You will arrive at the junction with the Crawford Mountain Trail at 9.1 km (5.7 mi.).

CRAWFORD MOUNTAIN TRAIL

Length: 2.7 kilometers (1.7 miles)
Direction of travel: Northeast
Difficulty: Moderate
Elevation: 818–1,150 meters (2,681–3,770 feet)
Difference in elevation: 332 meters (1,089 feet)
Markings: Yellow plastic diamonds
Trail #: 443
How to get there: To reach the Crawford Mountain Trail, go through Buffalo Gap on Virginia Route 42 and turn right on County Road 688. Drive northwest for 6.1 km (3.8 mi.) to the trail on the north side of the road.

The other end of the trail can be reached via the Crawford Knob Trail.

Trail description: The trail ascends at a moderate rate from the road, which actually lies in a saddle between Crawford Mountain and its southern neighbor, Elliott Knob. This saddle is called Dry Branch Gap on the USGS map.

There is a lot of evidence of illegal ATV use on this trail; double treads and erosion detract somewhat from the pleasant experience of the hike. Throughout the trail a mixed hardwood forest prevails.

At 2.5 km (1.5 mi.) you will come to the unmarked terminus of the Chimney Hollow Trail on your left. The trail is obvious; you can hardly miss it.

Shortly thereafter you will reach the—again unmarked—junction with the Red Oak Spring Trail branching off to the right. Descending it 0.3 km (0.2 mi.) you will reach Red Oak Spring. This side trail is very hard to find unless you already know where it is.

The Crawford Mountain Trail continues to ascend. At 2.7 km (1.7 mi.), not long after the Red Oak Spring Trail, you will come to the junction with the Crawford Knob Trail. This junction is well marked. Here you will have to turn and follow the Crawford Knob Trail down to the road.

The Crawford Mountain Trail continues straight ahead and shortly passes over the summit of Crawford Mountain. It runs through public lands for a while, but it eventually dead-ends at private land. Due to the revocation of the access privilege through this private land on U.S. 250, you must now either backtrack your steps the entire length of the Crawford Mountain Trail or turn off at the junction with the Crawford Knob Trail or the Chimney Hollow Trail and hike down one of them.

CHIMNEY HOLLOW TRAIL

Length: 5.8 kilometers (3.6 miles)
Direction of travel: South
Difficulty: Moderate
Elevation: 590–1,113 meters (1,935–3,650 feet)
Difference in elevation: 523 meters (1,714 feet)
Markings: Yellow plastic diamonds
Trail #: 487
How to get there: Go 29.6 km (18.4 mi.) west from Staunton on

U.S. 250. Watch for the trail sign a few hundred meters after the highway reaches a height-of-land marked NORTH MOUNTAIN. Park along the side of the road. The trail leaves on the south side.

You can reach the other end of the trail from the Crawford Mountain Trail.

Trail description: At first the trail ascends gradually through the beautiful ravine of Chimney Hollow. Large hemlocks, white pines, and rhododendron grow in this narrow valley, setting it apart from the area's usual oak woods.

After 2.3 km (1.4 mi.) you will reach the head of the ravine. There are a number of beautiful views all along this trail.

The trail now turns aside to skirt Coalpit Knob, a prominent outlier of the main Crawford Mountain ridge (elevation: 867 m; 2,841 ft.). If you wish to ascend the knob, you will have to bushwhack.

After rounding Coalpit Knob, the trail follows the connecting ridge. Oaks dominate the vegetation along this section of the trail.

At length the trail climbs the main Crawford Mountain ridge with one switchback to the left—avoid the faint trail to the right. On top of the ridge the Chimney Hollow Trail ends after 5.8 km (3.6 mi.), at the Crawford Mountain Trail.

5
Elliott Knob Area

Elliott Knob, at 1,361 meters (4,463 feet), is the highest elevation in the George Washington National Forest. Like its neighbor to the immediate north, Crawford Mountain, Elliott Knob is located in Augusta County.

Elliott Knob consists of a mountain ridge and its outliers and considerable lower land, especially to the northwest side. On the ridge is a peak with the highest elevation in the forest: This, strictly speaking, is Elliott Knob. The rest of the ridge is Great North Mountain. Common usage, though, refers to the entire ridge as Elliott Knob, and we do likewise.

Few, if any, settlers appeared in the early history of Elliott Knob. Most of the area seems always to have been forest, although some evidence indicated clearing on the upper east face of the mountain before U.S. Forest Service acquisition. These places, which originally may have been highland pastures, have not recovered well. The mountain's west side shows considerable evidence of clear-cutting at the lower levels, where there is also an extensive network of interconnected game clearings.

Forest Service plans call for continued timber harvest by clear-cutting. A timber sale has taken place off the Falls Hollow Trail. The logging road is closed now that the operation is complete. A small parking area for hikers has also been constructed off Virginia Route 42.

A fire tower is located atop the peak. An access road, which is closed to vehicles, leads to it from the east. There is no public access to the tower—the gate at the bottom and the trapdoor on top are both locked. Just below the mountain's summit on the east side is a large and unsightly UHF television transmission tower.

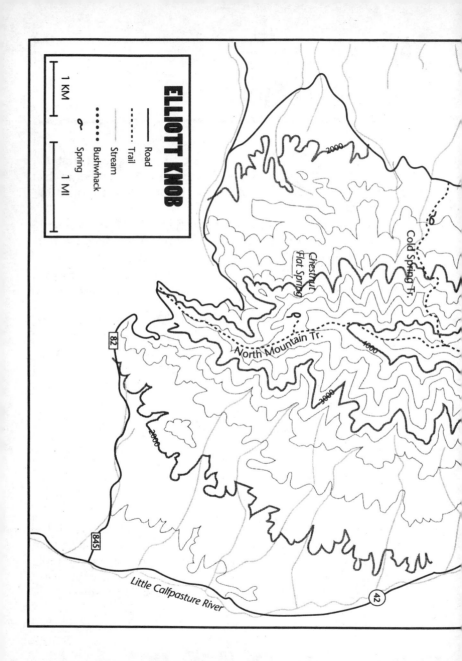

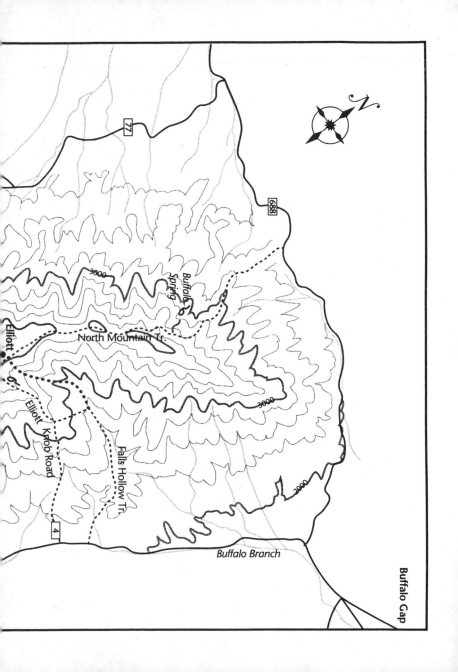

This mountain is generally higher, steeper, and more spectacular than Crawford Mountain. Despite the insults visited upon it, it remains a splendid peak. The entire west side of the main ridge, as well as its outliers, is particularly scenic and unspoiled, with magnificent stands of timber in its steep coves. The flora of these coves has a more northerly aspect than that of the remainder of the mountain. Among others we have found wildflowers such as lady slippers, bleeding hearts, trillium, violets, and dwarf iris. But botanical surprises can be found anywhere, and many high places on the upper flanks are only imperfectly known.

Elliott Knob, like Crawford Mountain, tends to be dry, with few active streams and only four developed springs. There are several excellent views from Elliott Knob itself and along the North Mountain Trail.

The climate is generally mild, similar to the climate of Crawford Mountain. Temperatures in summer as well as in winter are below those of the lowlands. Be prepared for freezing weather in winter.

No camping or fire permits are necessary on Elliott Knob.

The Deerfield Ranger District has marked foot trails in non-wilderness areas with yellow plastic diamonds.

Maps: USGS Elliott Knob and Augusta Springs quadrangles, 7.5 minute series; Deerfield Ranger District map, George Washington National Forest.

ELLIOTT KNOB ROAD

Length: 4.7 kilometers (2.9 miles)
Direction of travel: Generally west
Difficulty: Moderate to strenuous
Elevation: 648–1,361 meters (2,125–4,463 feet)
Difference in elevation: 713 meters (2,338 feet)
Markings: None needed
Trail #: 444

How to get there: The trail starts 5.3 km (3.3 mi.) south of Buffalo Gap on Virginia Route 42. The road is gated, but there is room enough to park maybe two cars without blocking the gate itself. There is no sign at the entrance or on the road.

This road offers direct access to the summit of Elliott Knob from the east.

Trail description: The trail is actually a broad gravel road that takes a straightforward ridge-top route all the way to the summit and is something of a long pull in sunny, hot weather. It passes almost from beginning to end through tracts of head-high scrub of pine, oak, and laurel, indicative of past clearing. This makes for good views back over the Shenandoah valley and, unfortunately, for a prostrating absence of shade. The road itself has somewhat treacherous footing (loose gravel), so watch your step carefully.

At about 2.4 km (1.5 mi.) you will reach the junction with the Falls Hollow Trail on your right. A power line runs overhead, and the intersection is marked with a yellow plastic diamond and a sign, which may well have disappeared by the time you get there.

On the right, after 3.9 km (2.4 mi.), you will see a small pond. Just above this pond are two springs. The spring farthest from the road has been boxed in with a wooden access door, and a plastic pipe discharges the water. An old apple tree and two tamarack trees grow here, with turkey beard and cinnamon ferns on the ground below.

At 4.7 km (2.9 mi.) you will reach the partly cleared summit (1,361 m; 4,463 ft.), with its fringe of planted spruce and larch and its fire tower. No public access to the tower exists; it is gated and locked. This is the highest point in George Washington National Forest.

FALLS HOLLOW TRAIL

Length: 3.7 kilometers (2.3 miles); add 1.4 kilometers (0.9 mile) for bushwhacking to North Mountain Trail
Direction of travel: Generally west
Difficulty: Strenuous
Elevation: 612–1,281 meters (2,008–4,200 feet)
Difference in elevation: 669 meters (2,192 feet)
Markings: Yellow plastic diamonds
Trail #: 657
How to get there: Drive 4.8 km (3 mi.) south of Buffalo Gap on Virginia Route 42 until you come to a road on the right marked 291. There are no other signs here or at the trailhead. Turn onto a black-topped apron which will almost immediately become a gravel road. Go a short distance to the small parking area (four or five cars) at a gated road. Just past this road are the ruins of an old brick house, and a bit farther on is the beginning of Elliott Knob Road.
Trail description: The trail passes through a very beautiful mountain hollow, where mature hemlock, linden, and birch tower above the falls and pools of a charming brook.

Start your hike by following the road beyond the gate. The new logging road follows the old trail fairly closely and occasionally you will see an old yellow blaze.

Passing at first over low ridges, the trail threads through an extensive area of game clearings, affording some views of the higher ridges ahead. A clear-cut has been completed recently, and the scars are likely to remain visible for a few years.

Four logging roads go off to the right with no markings of any kind. This area can be a bit confusing. Stay on the old woods road, which is fairly distinguishable from the new logging roads.

At 2.4 km (1.5 mi.) the path picks up the little brook—Buffalo Branch—for the first time near a small cascade and proceeds uphill through an increasingly narrow gorge, never far from the stream. The forest scenery is impressive.

The trail crosses the brook twice. Since the trail is very obscure here, when in doubt, follow the stream. At 3.7 km (2.3 mi.) the trail crosses the creek a third time and then begins to disintegrate rapidly. Shortly, you will find two small waterfalls to your right.

Just past the second fall, the trail turns left. The turn is marked by a yellow diamond plastic marker. The trail beyond this point is in good condition and easy to follow along a gentle grade around the mountain.

Approximately 1.6 km (1 mi.) later you will reach the junction with Elliott Knob Road. The junction is again marked with a plastic yellow diamond and a sign leaning against its disintegrating post, though it may well have disappeared by the time you get there.

Turn right on Elliott Knob Road to reach the summit in approximately 2.4 km (1.5 mi.). A left turn and another 2.4 km (1.5 mi.) will bring you back to Route 42.

If you prefer to bushwhack up along the creek, do not turn left beyond the small waterfalls. Continue following the creek until, after 1.4 km (0.9 mi.) more of scrambling up the hollow, you arrive at the North Mountain Trail near the summit. Watch carefully for the narrow footpath.

A left turn onto the North Mountain Trail will take you to the Elliott Knob Road. Turn right onto the road, and in 0.5 km (0.3 mi.) you will reach the summit and fire tower.

NORTH MOUNTAIN TRAIL

Length: 14.2 kilometers (8.8 miles)
Direction of travel: Generally southwest
Difficulty: Moderate
Elevation: 818–1,300–970 meters (2,681–4,263– 3,182 feet)

Difference in elevation: 482–330 meters (1,582–1,081 feet)
Markings: Yellow plastic diamonds
Trail #: 443
How to get there: Just south of Buffalo Gap on Virginia Route 42, turn right onto County Road 688, which is at first paved, then gravel, and proceed 6.1 km (3.8 mi.) to the height-of-land between Elliott Knob and Crawford Mountain. Parking can be found on the south side of the road. The gated North Mountain Trail goes south and uphill from the parking area. This trail is a southern continuation of the Crawford Mountain Trail. The trail here is also called Elliott Knob Trail on some maps.

To get to the other end of the trail, follow Route 42 until 12.9 km (8 mi.) south of Buffalo Gap. Just past the village of Augusta Springs, you can see Forest Development Road 845 (gravel) on the right, with a post marking the road number. This road later turns into FDR 82. It is 7.2 km (4.5 mi.) to the height-of-land, whence the gated North Mountain Trail goes steeply uphill to the right.

Trail description: Leaving the parking area, the North Mountain Trail ascends what is really an extended ridge side of Elliott Knob. At 0.3 km (0.2 mi.) from the parking area, the trail drops from the ridge to the right to avoid posted private property. The well-graded detour regains the ridge at 1.3 km (0.8 mi.). Then the trail climbs in step-wise fashion through pleasant woods.

Reaching steeper slopes at 2.4 km (1.5 mi.), the trail turns aside from its ridge to climb across and around the buttress ridges of the mountain's upper flank, never very steeply. Including the original ridge, four such buttresses are rounded. Their dry southwestern sides are sparsely vegetated, offering both plentiful blueberries in season and many grand views up the summit ridge and down to the southwest over spectacular terrain to the Deerfield valley, with Shenandoah Mountain beyond. In the coves you will see magnificent forest growth.

On rounding the second ridge at 3.4 km (2.1 mi.), you will see an unmarked trail branching off to the right and downhill. This trail descends 0.3 km (0.2 mi.) to Buffalo Spring. Another trail branches off to the right 300 m after the trail to Buffalo Spring. It peters out shortly, so stay to the left.

At 4.8 km (3 mi.) the main trail attains the summit ridge and continues along it through woods for 0.3 km (0.2 mi.), before dropping off slightly to the left to round a minor peak.

Leaving the trail here and bushwhacking straight ahead a short distance to the top of the peak will reveal a large rock outcrop on the peak's west side, which affords superb views.

Shortly after regaining the ridge top, the North Mountain Trail again slabs left to join the Elliott Knob Road at 7.6 km (4.7 mi.), 0.6 km (0.4 mi.) below the summit. Springs can be found a short distance left and down the road.

Turning right onto the road and following it up 0.3 km (0.2 mi.), you will find a trail with yellow markers turning off to the left. Take this trail to continue southwest along the summit ridge. (Elliott Knob Road goes on to the right and upward to the peak, where you can obtain excellent views of the surrounding countryside.)

At 0.2 km (0.1 mi.) past the junction, the Cold Spring Trail branches off to the right. A sign will mark the location for you.

About 0.5 km (0.3 mi.) farther on, the trail climbs out of the woods onto the so-called "Hogback," a secondary summit of the mountain (1,356 m; 4,447 ft.)—cleared during World War II as a potential navy radar site and now for the most part overgrown with scrub. Some views are afforded by scattered rockslides. Here, also, the trail widens to a rough jeep road.

Reentering the woods, the road descends gradually along the ridge. The last 5 km (3 mi.) or so may become rather overgrown in summer. You may consider wearing long pants for this hike.

At 11.3 km (7 mi.) from the trailhead, a side trail leaves on the right, which leads to the Chestnut Flat Spring after an easy walk of 0.5 km (0.3 mi.).

At 14.2 km (8.8 mi.) the road ends at FDR 82—Hite Hollow Road—in a slight gap (970 m; 3,182 ft.).

If you hike the trail in the opposite direction, watch for the left turn of the North Mountain Trail off the Elliott Knob Road just above a power line pole. A post with yellow markers indicates the location of the trailhead, which is rather overgrown here.

COLD SPRING TRAIL

Length: 3.9 kilometers (2.4 miles)
Direction of travel: Generally east
Difficulty: Moderate to strenuous
Elevation: 729–1,312 meters (2,390–4,300 feet)
Difference in elevation: 583 meters (1,910 feet)
Markings: Yellow plastic diamonds
Trail #: 445
How to get there: Go south of Buffalo Gap on Virginia Route 42, and turn right onto County Road 688, which is at first paved, then gravel. Go about 9.3 km (5.8 mi.)—3.2 km (2 mi.) past the height-of-land between Crawford Mountain and Elliott Knob and the start of the North Mountain Trail—to the junction with a good gravel road, Forest Development Road 77, on the left. The signs read TO HITE HOLLOW ROAD. Turn here. Make sure you do not take a road branching to the right from FDR 77 at 4.7 km (2.9 mi.). At 5.6 km (3.5 mi.) you will see a woods road on the left, accompanied by a sign on the right, with lettering on the reverse side only reading EL-LIOTT KNOB TRAIL: ELLIOTT KNOB L. O. 3.2 KM (2 MI.). The woods road is passable by car for several hundred meters but is then reduced to a footpath. Park your car.

This trail offers access to the summit of Elliott Knob from the west.

Trail description: The trail almost immediately crosses a small brook, Still Run, and then follows it on the right. Sixty to seventy paces after the crossing, depending upon your length of step, the trail rather obscurely turns right and away from the brook.

Turn left and look for yellow markers. The road is quite over-grown. A spruce grove will be on the right side of the road, and just past it there are superb blackberries in early August.

The so-called "Cold Spring" lies about 50 m south of the path, on a short but unmarked and overgrown side trail. You may have trouble locating the spring, but many hikers claim it is easily found and it is a source of water (treat before using). To find the spring, you may want to watch for evidence of camping and, just below the spring where the soil is moist, for tall (1.2 to 1.5 m or 4 to 5 ft.) cinnamon ferns growing in profusion.

Soon the road narrows into a good graded trail and ascends via one of the mountain's many subsidiary ridges through pleasant woods. It then slabs across two adjoining ridges and makes an ascending traverse of the mountain's upper flank. The trail here passes through beautiful yellow birch woods and becomes considerably overgrown in summer.

The trail gains the summit ridge at 3.9 km (2.4 mi.) and ends at the North Mountain Trail. A sign marks the trailhead.

From here, turn left to reach the gravel Elliott Knob Road in 0.2 km (0.1 mi.), which in turn leads left to the summit in another 0.3 km (0.2 mi.).

6
Saint Mary's Wilderness

The Saint Mary's Wilderness lies on the west side of the Blue Ridge Mountains. Established by Congress in 1984, the designated wilderness area includes only the drainage of the Saint Mary's River, a total of 40.8 square kilometers (10,090 acres). We have also included trails outside the wilderness itself on the massif. While some circuit hikes require walking along stretches of road, they usually make up for it with some scenic spots or views.

We have taken the following roads as boundaries for the area we describe: County roads 664, 608, and 814; Forest Development Road 42; State Route 56, and the Blue Ridge Parkway. Only one trail lies outside these roads: the White Rock Falls Trail.

The region was extensively mined and logged during the last century. You can find a number of old mines and slag hills throughout the region. The trees were converted to charcoal to feed the furnaces. Mount Torry Furnace, on Route 664 near the entrance to the Sherando Lake Campground, is well preserved. American Indians and later settlers lived in the valleys around the region, but probably never on the mountain itself.

The forest has recovered nicely from the logging, and the area is generally deeply forested. The trees are mainly hardwoods with occasional evergreens, mostly hemlocks, near streams. Azaleas and rhododendron grow throughout the region. Along FDR 42 we found a number of fringe trees blooming in late May. Some wildflowers can be found in spots.

Bears do exist here—we saw one along Mills Creek Trail in May—but are extremely shy, and so are the deer. In addition, squirrels, raccoons, skunks, and other small mammals populate the region. Birds are plentiful, both migrants and year-round residents.

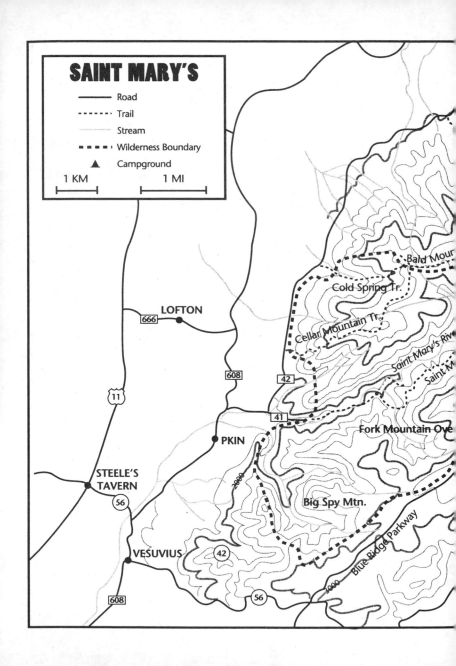

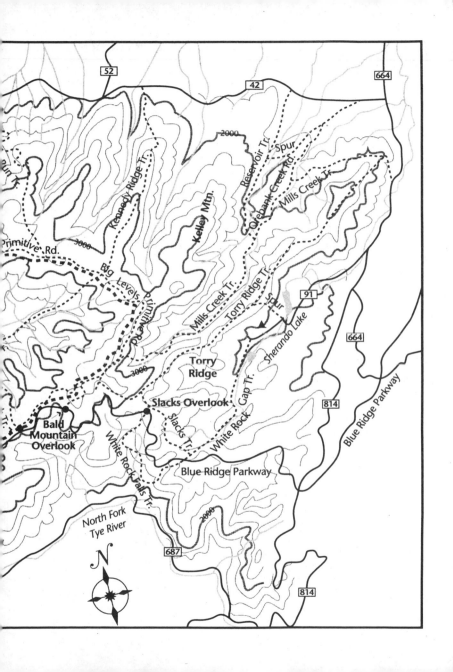

As there is a fair amount of water around, voracious mosquitoes also frequent certain areas.

Many trails start out as hunter access roads, rather broad and frequently deeply rutted woods roads which often become true trails later on. Some have berms, others are gated. Only the Bald Mountain and Big Levels Primitive roads are wide enough for two vehicles to pass each other easily. These two roads, which run along the top of the plateau, are also somewhat boring, and in summer, hot and dusty. Of course, no mountain bikes or other mechanized equipment are allowed within the Saint Mary's Wilderness.

In the fall hunters abound—first bear hunters with their many dogs, later deer and turkey hunters roam on all trails. If you are planning to hike then, make sure you wear some blaze orange and avoid light-colored clothing that might be mistaken for the tail of a deer.

There are a number of good campsites throughout the area for backpackers and car campers alike. Sherando Lake Campground is run by the Forest Service and you have to pay a daily fee to stay there. There are two nice lakes—the lower one has a beach. Showers are available in the bathhouse, and running water is provided throughout the campground. The lower lake was built by the Civilian Conservation Corps during the 1930s (.09 square kilometers; 22 acres), the smaller upper lake was built later for flood control. Off-road camping is available, particularly along FDR 42. If you walk or drive a bit along the hunter access roads, you can find many good spots.

If you plan a winter camping or hiking trip to the area, do check with the Forest Service first. Some of the forest development roads may be closed for several months, and the campground probably is, too.

Campfires are generally permitted except along either side of the Saint Mary's Trail from the parking lot on FDR 41 to 150 meters (500 feet) beyond the falls; building or maintaining a campfire in this area is prohibited. Camping is not allowed within 100 meters of FDR 41.

This area has many good circuit hikes, especially if you are willing to walk along a Forest Service road for a bit. Look at the map and the trail descriptions and find some trails that suit you and your abilities.

Maps: USGS Vesuvius and Big Levels quadrangles, 7.5 minute series; Pedlar Ranger District map, Saint Mary's Wilderness map, George Washington National Forest.

SAINT MARY'S TRAIL

Length: 10.5 kilometers (6.5 miles)

Direction of travel: East

Difficulty: Moderate

Elevation: 537–976 meters (1,760–3,200 feet)

Difference in elevation: 439 meters (1,440 feet)

Markings: Blue blazes

Trail #: 500

How to get there: From the town of Steele's Tavern, take State Route 56 south for 1.6 km (1 mi.). Go left on County Road 608. Shortly after passing under the railroad, go right on Forest Development Road 41, and drive to the parking lot at its end.

The other end of the trail can be reached via the Big Levels Primitive Road.

Trail description: At the parking lot start your hike at the gate, which has a sign indicating that you are about to enter the Saint Mary's River Wilderness Area.

The trail follows the stream closely at first. There are a number of nice campsites along this stretch. The trail is fairly rocky, and you will have to watch your footing.

Watch for the trail as it makes a number of turns. About 1.6 km (1 mi.) from the start you will have to cross the Saint Mary's River.

After another 0.8 km (0.5 mi.) you will reach a trail junction. Just before this junction the trail will lead you along some narrow ledges about 3 m above the river. Be careful walking along here as the footing is treacherous in places.

At the junction, straight ahead is a spur trail leading to a waterfall on the Saint Mary's River, while the main Saint Mary's Trail turns right and uphill.

Following the spur trail, cross the Saint Mary's River (you will have to wade to get to the other side) and walk along an old woods road, which actually may have been a railroad grade once. Follow this path, which runs close to the river through some beautiful spots with rhododendron hanging over the water. There are some nice swimming holes here.

You will have to cross the river several times, but after about 0.8 km (0.5 mi.) you will reach a beautiful campsite under a towering cliff. The campsite is on a wide ledge and drops off a bit toward the river. Just a few meters beyond are the falls. The scenery is well worth the hike.

Back at the junction with the Saint Mary's Trail, take the right fork uphill. For a short stretch you will follow Sugartree Branch, a tributary of the Saint Mary's River. Again, this is a very pretty section, and you will want to have your camera ready.

About 0.5 km (0.3 mi.) up Sugartree Branch, the trail crosses the tributary and goes steeply uphill. The right fork of the trail leads to the remains of a fairly large old mine. As always, exercise caution and common sense when exploring around old mines or buildings.

Bear left to follow the main trail. The walking is fairly level here through deciduous woods with much undergrowth. Roughly 1.6 km (1 mi.) from the first mine, you will come across the remains of another, smaller one. A few meters beyond you will reach the intersection with the Mine Bank Trail, which ascends the mountain to the right. There is a flat area around the old mine where you might camp.

Just after this intersection, cross the Mine Bank Creek. With a minor up-and-down the trail becomes level for a while. There are some big rhododendron around, which should look beautiful in bloom.

There are several more creek crossings ahead. After the last one, the trail becomes rocky and begins to ascend, sometimes rather steeply, towards Green Pond and the Big Levels. The large trees become intermittent and much of the vegetation looks rather scrubby. There are lots of blueberry bushes, though, and the harvest should be good in season.

At 9.7 km (6 mi.) the climb ends where the trail reaches the Big Levels area. The trail splits in two here—take either one to reach the Big Levels Primitive Road. A little side trail leads to Green Pond, which is surrounded by marsh.

At 10.5 km (6.5 mi.) from the parking lot, you will reach the boundary of the Saint Mary's Wilderness. A sign and a gate mark the end of Saint Mary's Trail. Straight ahead is the Kennedy Ridge Trail, and the Big Levels Primitive Road is to the left and right.

MINE BANK TRAIL

Length: 3.4 kilometers (2.1 miles)
Direction of travel: South
Difficulty: Moderate
Elevation: 671–1,003 meters (2,200–3,290 feet)
Difference in elevation: 332 meters (1,090 feet)
Markings: Orange blazes
Trail #: 500C
How to get there: Via the Saint Mary's or Bald Mountain trails.
Trail description: Leaving from its starting point on the Saint Mary's Trail, at first the trail ascends slowly at a distance from Mine Bank Creek, but it soon approaches the creek, following its bed closely most of the time and crossing and recrossing it.

The trail soon starts climbing more steeply. The trees are primarily deciduous with some evergreens, mostly hemlock. The understory has some large rhododendron growing in the ravine.

The trail is occasionally obstructed by fallen logs, which could prove a bit tricky to negotiate. The closeness of the stream and general moist character of the area could make some of the rockier parts of the trail slippery.

There are quite a few interesting ledges and rocky outcrops along the path, which make for picturesque views. Higher up in the ravine you will find a beautiful stand of hemlocks together with some large rhododendron.

After one steep section a faint trail leads straight ahead. Stay on the main trail to the left.

After another steep climb out of the valley, the trail levels somewhat. Here it leads through a younger forest, leaving the big hemlocks behind. Soon it reaches its junction with the Bald Mountain Trail. A few meters farther is the trailhead near the Fork Mountain Overlook on the Blue Ridge Parkway.

CELLAR MOUNTAIN TRAIL

Length: 4.7 kilometers (2.9 miles)
Direction of travel: Generally east
Difficulty: Moderate
Elevation: 622–1,104–1,031 meters (2,040–3,620–3,380 feet)
Difference in elevation: 482–73 meters (1,580–240 feet)
Markings: Blue blazes
Trail #: 501
How to get there: From Steele's Tavern, take State Route 56 south. Go left on County Road 608. Shortly after passing under the railroad, go right on Forest Development Road 41 and then left on FDR 42. The trail leaves from a small parking area, 1.6 km (1 mi.) after the turn onto FDR 42.

The other end of the trail can be reached via the Bald Mountain Primitive Road and the Cold Spring Trail.
Trail description: The trail starts at the gate just beyond the intersection with FDR 42. It lies within the Saint Mary's Wilderness.

The trail immediately starts its climb toward the top. After 0.4 km (0.2 mi.) you will encounter a small stream, which can be crossed without difficulty. Its spring is on the left just off the trail.

Ascending more or less straight up the ridge without any real switchbacks, the trail is fairly steep at times. If you look back every so often, you will have nice views over the valley, especially during the early part of the hike.

There are several large anthills beside the trail. The forest here is scrubby brush with only small trees. The absence of shade will probably make for a hot hike in the summer, but blueberry plants like it and they will provide you with a nice snack in season. Later on there are a few bigger pines and partial shade.

About halfway up the trail, you will have a view of Cellar Mountain. There are some nice rocks to the right of the trail. A possible campsite exists here, but you will have to bring in your own water.

A steeper part of the trail follows. We found lots of lilies-of-the-valley blooming here in late May. Soon the trail passes over a saddle, descends a bit, then starts going up again. You will find a fork in the trail—the right branch gets progressively fainter, so stay to the left. Gypsy moths have been at work in this part of the forest, and there are a number of dead and dying trees around.

The trail now descends from the top of the mountain, at times steeply, then flattens a bit. Here is a beautiful area of large rhododendron and mountain laurel, which are just coming into bloom in late May. At times the trail is a bit rocky, so watch your footing carefully.

At 5.3 km (3.3 mi.) the trail ends at a gate. Just beyond is the Bald Mountain Primitive Road, which ends here in a turnaround. The Cold Spring Trail starts a few meters to the left. Walking along the road, you will pass the upper ends of many of the other trails described in this chapter, and eventually you will arrive at the Bald Mountain Overlook on the Blue Ridge Parkway.

COLD SPRING TRAIL

Length: 3.9 kilometers (1.8 miles)
Direction of travel: West
Difficulty: Moderate
Elevation: 634–1,031 meters (2,080–3,380 feet)
Difference in elevation: 397 meters (1,300 feet)
Markings: None, trail easy to follow
Trail #: None
How to get there: Via the Bald Mountain Primitive Road or the Cellar Mountain Trail.

The other end of the trail can be reached from Steele's Tavern by taking State Route 56 south for 1.6 km (1 mi.) and turning left on County Road 608. Shortly after passing under the railroad, go right on Forest Development Road 41 and then turn left on FDR 42. After the last turn, it is 4.2 km (2.6 mi.) to the start of the Cold Spring Trail.

Trail description: The trailhead starts on the right side of the turn-around of the Bald Mountain Primitive Road. The beginning is not in the wilderness itself, but enters it shortly. The trail descends steeply downhill and is covered with loose rocks and pine needles, making the footing somewhat treacherous.

A number of switchbacks occur on this trail. The first of these gives some nice views over the valley, as the trees are not very large here. Along the side of the mountain, you will find lots of mountain laurel.

A spring runs across the trail; step across. The trail is still rocky, and you will see a stone slide shortly. Several switchbacks now follow upon each other's heels. The trail is more level now, but passes right across the slide. Sometimes you will have to contend with lots of greenbriar, which grabs at your clothes and legs.

After the rock slides, the trail again descends very steeply for a stretch. You will reach a stream, which you can hop across on stones. You are now on the valley floor, and the trail descends more gently, becoming an old woods road. Follow it along the stream, which you will have to cross again. Soon you will also encounter a large wet area with a side stream across the trail. You should have little trouble finding a way around and across without taking off your shoes.

A short level stretch will bring you to a gate, which marks the wilderness boundary. A bit further along is a Forest Service steel gate barring access for motorized vehicles. The trail ends on FDR 42, just opposite a dirt road, which is posted.

It is 2.6 km (1.6 mi.) to the left on FDR 42 and 41 to the parking lot for the Cellar Mountain Trail.

BALD MOUNTAIN TRAIL

Length: 3.5 kilometers (2.2 miles)
Direction of travel: East
Difficulty: Moderate
Elevation: 854–1,055 meters (2,800–3,460 feet)
Difference in elevation: 201 meters (660 feet)
Markings: Infrequent yellow blazes
Trail #: 500F
How to get there: The trail starts from a parking area just south of the Fork Mountain Overlook, shortly after Milepost 22 on the Blue Ridge Parkway.

The other end can be reached via the Bald Mountain and Big Levels primitive roads.

Trail description: Begin walking the trail at the back of the parking lot, and watch out for a fork in the trail; the Bald Mountain Trail turns right, while the Mine Bank Trail continues straight ahead. A cairn indicates the turn.

The trail is an old woods road that goes downhill gently but steadily. In a moist area, about 1.6 km (1 mi.) from the start, quite a few different kinds of fern grow as well as rhododendron and hemlocks. A small stream, possibly dry in summer, flows close by.

Soon thereafter are three more stream crossings. These have logs across them and are easy to pass. On the right you will now come to a pretty little waterfall. Again, it probably does not carry enough water to last through summer. Shortly after this comes the fourth stream crossing.

The trail is alternately grassy and mossy with many hemlocks in spots. There is a nice campsite close by the next stream, where the trail becomes rather faint.

Ignore a small path to the side and stay on the main trail, which now starts going uphill a bit more steeply. As you gain altitude the woods become more open, and are again filled with ferns. Another small stream, this one with a little cascade, flows next to the trail. A grove of large hemlocks surrounds this spot.

The trail now turns right and crosses and recrosses a creek. Every so often you can find a faint yellow blaze, and unless the Forest Service has done some maintenance recently, you will have to watch carefully. The creek crossings are somewhat difficult at times, mostly due to fallen trees. There is a very large hemlock in this area—we needed three people to measure its circumference of about 3 m (9 ft.).

Leave the stream and cross a rocky spot, going fairly steeply uphill. The trail moderates its climb, but still remains somewhat rocky. We found many lilies-of-the-valley growing here.

The Bald Mountain Trail ends at a bend of the Big Levels Primitive Road.

BIG LEVELS-BALD MOUNTAIN PRIMITIVE ROAD

Length: 11.6 kilometers (7.2 miles)
Direction of travel: North and west
Difficulty: Easy
Elevation: 982–1,067 meters (3,220–3,500 feet)
Difference in elevation: 85 meters (280 feet)
Markings: None needed
FDR #: 162
How to get there: Park on the Bald Mountain Overlook on the Blue Ridge Parkway, shortly after milepost 22.
Trail description: This is a primitive woods road that skirts around the wilderness area. It provides access for hunters to the eastern part of the area, which is not included in the officially designated wilderness.

During the summer it is a fairly hot hike, as there is not much shade along the way. Most of the vegetation along the sides is just scrubby brush, especially during the ascent to the Big Levels from the parkway. At times it is also fairly steep.

The Big Levels Primitive Road leaves from the Bald Mountain

Overlook and climbs gently. At 1.1 km (0.7 mi.) the Bald Mountain Trail comes in on the left, and at 1.8 km (1.1 mi.) from the Bald Mountain Overlook, a spur road branches right to a radio tower on the summit of Bald Mountain. The Torry Ridge Trail starts from this spur road shortly before the tower.

There is a clearing on the right at the junction with the Mills Creek Trail (blue blazes). This point is 2.3 km (1.4 mi.) from the Bald Mountain Overlook, and from here it is 3.9 km (2.4 mi.) to Saint Mary's and Kennedy Ridge trails. Stony Run is 5.8 km (3.6 mi.) distant, and Cold Spring and Cellar Mountain are at 8.5 km (5.3 mi.). As this old road skirts the wilderness boundary, every so often you may find a wilderness sign on the left.

The ascent to Flint Mountain and the descent to Big Levels are fairly steep. Just before the top you will see a water drain on the right and a foot trail. This trail leads to some small rock outcrops with nice views over Kennedy Creek.

After you have reached the top of Flint Mountain, continue along the road for a while until you come to a four-way intersection with a fairly large clearing. On the right is the Kennedy Ridge Trail, which leads to Route 42. On the left you will find a gate and the entrance to the Saint Mary's Trail. Straight ahead the primitive road continues. It is an easy hike with few ups and downs.

After a while you will again start a small rise and near the top come to a slimy pond on the left. Shortly thereafter you will come to the junction with the Stony Run Trail on the right (8 km; 5 mi.). Here the Big Levels Primitive Road changes its name to Bald Mountain Primitive Road.

Now you will again encounter a rise. Beyond the top is a frog pond on the left with a campsite beside it. A few meters later, a side road on the right goes 200 m to a dead end at another campsite.

Continue on the road until it forks. The right hand branch runs about 0.8 km (0.5 mi.) amid scrubby vegetation and dead-ends with no views. Take the left hand branch of the road, which ends in a turnaround after about 100 m. Here you will find the trailheads for the Cellar Mountain and Cold Spring trails.

STONY RUN TRAIL

Length: 8 kilometers (5 miles)
Direction of travel: South
Difficulty: Moderate
Elevation: 586–1,000 meters (1,920–3,280 feet)
Difference in elevation: 414 meters (1,360 feet)
Markings: None needed
Trail #: None
How to get there: From Sherando take County Road 664 south and turn right onto Forest Development Road 42. Follow this for 10.9 km (6.8 mi.) to a wide spot in the road, from which the Stony Run Trail leaves on the left as a rough jeep road.
Trail description: The road starts going uphill to the left. About 100 m later a sign warns you that this is a "narrow rough road," and 20 m farther there is a gate, which is probably open only during hunting season. Almost immediately thereafter comes the first switchback.

This trail climbs steadily up the ridge via innumerable switchbacks. If you take these, the trail ascends gently and is fairly pleasant. Unfortunately, a shortcut that bypasses most of these switchbacks has become established—a horribly steep, stony, and rough road that goes almost vertically up the hill. We recommend strongly that you avoid this path and follow the switchbacks.

After the seventh or eighth switchback, this stony cut-off road ends, and within a few hundred meters there is a short spur trail to the left, which leads to a campsite with a good view into the deep gulch of John's Run. Shortly after this junction you will find another spur trail, this time to the right, which leads, after about 50 m, to a parallel, but smaller road.

Now you will come to a spot with nice views to the left into the gulch. The junction with the smaller road is just ahead to the left (if you are hiking this trail downhill, keep to the right). This is the top of the ridge.

Continue on the trail, descending gradually toward the source of the creek. This water may dry up during the summer and fall, so do not rely on it when backpacking.

At 8 km (5 mi.) you will reach the end of the trail at a big intersection with several campsites. There are no signs to indicate this spot. To the right is the Bald Mountain Primitive Road, to the left the same road is called Big Levels Primitive Road.

KENNEDY RIDGE TRAIL

Length: 5.6 kilometers (3.5 miles)
Direction of travel: Southwest
Difficulty: Moderate
Elevation: 549–976 meters (1,800–3,200 feet)
Difference in elevation: 427 meters (1,400 feet)
Markings: None needed
Trail #: None
How to get there: From Sherando take County Road 664 south and turn right onto Forest Development Road 42. At 6.1 km (3.8 mi.) from County Road 664, you will see the Kennedy Ridge Trail entering the woods on your left.

The other end of the trail can be reached via the Big Levels Primitive Road at 3.9 km (2.4 mi.).

Trail description: The trail starts on the left side of Route 42. Once you enter the woods, you will almost immediately encounter a sign reading KENNEDY RIDGE TRAIL—GREEN POND 3.5.

The trail travels through pleasant pine woods. The walking is easy at first, but soon the trail becomes steeper, and in spots the walking is rather rough: There are lots of round stones, and the footing is difficult.

In general the trail ascends at a moderate rate, but there are a couple of spots where it climbs uphill more steeply. It alternates between a foot trail and an old woods road, but fortunately there is little evidence of recent vehicle use.

Shortly after the first steep ascent, you will top a narrow ridge.

To the right of the trail you will find some rocks, which provide a nice view, something not easily found on densely wooded slopes.

For a short stretch the trail descends steeply and again becomes a foot trail, covered with soft mosses and dirt. You may also find some forgotten old reddish-orange blazes here and there on trees.

Again a woods road, the trail now begins to climb steeply toward the Big Levels and then flattens out a bit. At 5.6 km (3.5 mi.) it reaches the Big Levels Primitive Road. To the right are the Bald Mountain Primitive Road and access to the Stony Run, Cold Spring, and Cellar Mountain trails. Straight ahead is the beginning of the Saint Mary's River Trail and Green Pond. To the left are the Mills Creek and Torry Ridge trails, the latter leading past the campground at Sherando Lake.

MILLS CREEK TRAIL

Length: 10.9 kilometers (6.8 miles)
Direction of travel: Generally west
Difficulty: Moderate
Elevation: 610–549–1,040 meters (2,000–1,800–3,440 feet)
Difference in elevation: 61–500 meters (200–1,640 feet)
Markings: Blue blazes
Trail #: 518
How to get there: Via the Torry Ridge Trail or the Bald Mountain Trail at the other end. A third approach to the middle of the trail is the Orebank Creek Road.
Trail description: The Mills Creek Trail starts on the Torry Ridge Trail where the latter makes a sharp turn. The turn and junction are marked with a double yellow blaze—there are no other obvious landmarks, so watch carefully.

The trail wanders along the hillside, fairly level for some time, then starts going downhill gently. The trees are not very dense, giving a relatively open feeling to the woods. The trail is a bit rocky here at times.

Just before the trail starts going a bit more steeply downhill and around a sharp right turn, you have somewhat of a view through the trees across the valley. Here we once saw a black bear sniffing among the underbrush.

After the trail turns sharply right, there is a deep gully on the left. The descent is a bit steeper now down the hillside. At the end of this descent, you will come to a junction with a well-used dirt road. The Mills Creek Trail turns left here. To the right, the road goes to a Civilian Conservation Corps Camp at Route 664. You may meet horses along this stretch of the trail.

Turning left you will immediately have to cross a small creek. Scramble a few meters up the trail, then start going downhill gently. Shortly you will come to another fork in the trail. The right branch is overgrown and disused. Follow the blue blazes to the left. The trail is a broad, level path here with quite a few blueberry bushes on either side. It is pleasant but uneventful hiking.

After 2.1 km (1.3 mi.) you will come to an intersection with an old woods road coming in from the left. You can follow the Mills Creek Trail straight ahead, but it passes through a boggy area more easily bypassed via the woods road. You can follow this to a clearing and second old woods road. Turn right at the second woods road, and the trail will go downhill steeply at the end of the clearing, meeting the Mills Creek Trail, coming in from the right at an indistinct junction.

A few meters beyond this junction is the crossing of Orebank Creek. During high water you may have to resort to wading. Here is the junction with the Orebank Creek Road to the right, which leads to Forest Development Road 42 in 2.4 km (1.5 mi.).

Some stones with blue blazes, as well as double blue diamonds on a tree, indicate the turn of Mills Creek Trail to the left. Pass a large berm and a few smaller ones and continue following an old woods road past several stony hillsides. These are probably old mines, and rough roads lead to some of them. You may want to do some exploring of your own; exercise common sense.

Negotiate additional berms farther along—they were placed

across the trail for runoff and probably also ATV control—before reaching a large meadow. Actually the meadowlike part starts a bit later. First you have to contend with thick bushes crowding in on the trail. These bushes are mostly autumn olives with bright red berries in the fall. Some birds like the berries, but the bushes are very prolific and are taking over fast.

Past the bushes the trail slopes gently downhill toward Mill Creek, following it for a brief stretch. Crossing the creek requires wading. Here you will find many wild grapevines, some of which bear fruit.

The trail continues on the other side of the creek, traveling along the left side. From a boggy spot in the trail about 100 m after crossing the creek, the Reservoir Trail leaves to the right, beyond a row of trees and up a step from where you are standing. The junction is very inconspicuous. A small clearing is beyond the trees, and walking through this you will find the Reservoir Trail.

Continue along the Mills Creek Trail, winding your way slowly uphill. Again this is an old woods road, which continues almost to the headwaters of Mills Creek before it turns into a true foot trail. The forest has many large trees in this area, most of them deciduous.

You will have to cross Mills Creek three more times. The woods road becomes a trail when it leaves the creek to begin its ascent toward the ridge. The trail now makes a sharp right turn and begins to climb a steep hillside via several switchbacks. It finally ends at the Bald Mountain and Big Levels Primitive Road.

TORRY RIDGE TRAIL

Length: 11.7 kilometers (7.3 miles)
Direction of travel: Generally east
Difficulty: Moderate
Elevation: 488–1,068 meters (1,600–3,500 feet)
Difference in elevation: 580 meters (1,900 feet)
Markings: Yellow blazes
Trail #: 507

How to get there: The Torry Ridge Trail can be reached via the Big Levels Primitive Road at 1.8 km (1.1 mi.). The other end of the trail is at Mount Torry Furnace, which is 4.3 km (2.7 mi.) south of Sherando on County Road 664.

Trail description: Near the remains of an old fire tower watch carefully for some yellow blazes indicating the beginning of the Torry Ridge Trail; the trailhead is not marked very well here. The trail starts on the left side of the spur of the road.

A true foot trail here, the trail starts out fairly level for a short stretch through scrubby woods, then starts its descent along the ridge. Later the trail leads through nice rhododendron thickets, which should look beautiful when they bloom. You will also find many blueberry bushes, which, in season, will provide sustenance for you if you stop along your hike. Mountain laurel can be found on the drier parts of the ridge.

The trail passes the end of a rock slide, which is to your left. Watch your footing among the rocks as you continue your hike downhill. At 1.9 km (1.2 mi.) you will reach the junction with the Slacks Trail, which turns right here toward the Sherando Lake area and reaches the White Rock Gap Trail in 3.5 km (2.2 mi.).

Continue straight along the Torry Ridge Trail, which descends gently but steadily. There are no views along this section of the trail.

About 3.1 km (1.9 mi.) later you will come to a spur trail leading down to the Sherando Lake campground in about 2.7 km (1.7 mi.). Walking down this trail will lead you to Lookout Rock in 0.8 km (0.5 mi.) via some switchbacks and stone steps, which moderate the descent. You will be rewarded with a great view over the valley, including Sherando Lake. This is a well-visited spot. The rest of the trail down to the campground is not quite as steep as above, though there are still some switchbacks and steps to be negotiated. You will reach the campground near a round water tower.

Back on the Torry Ridge Trail, continue straight ahead through the woods. With several ups and downs, the trail follows its downhill course steadily. At 6.4 km (4 mi.) the Blue Loop Trail intersects. This trail is made up of the spur trail described above, the Torry

Ridge Trail, and a trail beside Sherando Lake. While it does provide another nice view of the lake, it is extremely steep. It descends the mountain in 0.8 km (0.5 mi.) to the lake.

The Torry Ridge Trail continues on its course along the mountain. Through the trees you may get an occasional glimpse of the valley and surrounding mountains. The trail is rocky and steep at times. It meets the Mills Creek trail on the left at 10.1 km (6.3 mi.), just at the point where it makes a sharp right turn downhill toward its end at Route 664 at Mount Torry Furnace. A double blaze marks the junction with the Mills Creek Trail.

RESERVOIR TRAIL

Length: 4 kilometers (2.5 miles)
Direction of travel: South
Difficulty: Moderate
Elevation: 503–600 meters (1,650–1,970 feet)
Difference in elevation: 98 meters (320 feet)
Markings: None, generally easy to follow
Trail #: 518A (FDR 1234)
How to get there: From Sherando take County Road 664 south and turn right onto Forest Development Road 42. At 2.4 km (1.5 mi.) from County Road 664 the Reservoir Trail is on the left.

The other end can be reached via the Mills Creek Trail.

Trail description: Start your hike on FDR 1234, which is gated during most of the year, probably with the exception of hunting season. The road is fairly wide here. It climbs steadily toward the reservoir, but never very steeply. The woods on both sides are deep and shady.

About 1.6 km (1 mi.) after the gate, you will come upon the spur trail, on the left, to the Orebank Creek Road. No sign indicates the junction. Shortly after this you will arrive at the dam for a small reservoir. Stay on the right side and pass over the rise of the dam and through the dip behind it. Mostly grasses grow here.

After this grassy spot you will reach an open area under the trees (a possible campsite). The trail forks here: The right fork goes up a rise under the trees and eventually vanishes on the shoulder of Kelley Mountain; the left one follows the shoreline of the reservoir to its inlet. Here you have to turn left and cross the delta of the small creek that feeds the reservoir. This might provide you with a small problem after heavy rains or in the wet season. Wading may then be the only solution.

After having crossed the creek, turn toward the woods with your back to the lake and look for the continuation of the trail, which runs along an old woods road parallel to the creek. You may have to look a few feet to either side to find it. It is a very pleasant, fairly level hike through the woods.

Soon you will come to the banks of a creek. Follow it along the trail to the left. Here you will find some very pretty spots. A large rock wall is to the left, with a very nice, large campsite underneath.

Continue along the creek through the woods, and after a while you will come to a small gully with a creek flowing through it. Cross over a little to the left of the trail, and continue straight ahead on the other side. The trees recede, and you will walk along a broad, grassy area.

In about 0.3 km (0.2 mi.) you will reach the end of the grassy area and the end of the trail. Duck under the trees on the right and you will find yourself in the open area next to the Mills Creek Trail. Turn to the right and uphill along Mills Creek Trail and you will eventually reach Bald Mountain and Big Levels Primitive Road. If you turn left you will cross Mill Creek almost immediately and continue on downhill toward the Orebank Creek Road.

SLACKS TRAIL

Length: 3.5 kilometers (2.2 miles)
Direction of travel: South
Difficulty: Easy

Elevation: 869–701 meters (2,850–2,300 feet)
Difference in elevation: 168 meters (550 feet)
Markings: Blue blazes
Trail #: 480
How to get there: You can reach one end from the Torry Ridge Trail and the other via the White Rock Gap Trail. A third access to the trail is from the Slacks Overlook near Milepost 19 on the Blue Ridge Parkway. The orange-blazed spur trails leave from both ends of the parking lot.

Trail description: The sign at the Torry Ridge Trail points you down the Slacks Trail by telling you that it is 3.5 km (2.2 mi.) to the White Rock Gap Trail.

The trail leads downhill, and you will soon come upon a rock slide. Watch out for poison ivy growing among the rocks. When you have barely left one rock slide behind you, another will be waiting straight ahead. On the other side of the second slide, you will find a burned-over area, the result of a small wildfire that occurred rather recently.

The junction with the orange-blazed spur trail to the Slacks Overlook on the Blue Ridge Parkway is just ahead. The spur trail leaves to the right; there are no trail signs here.

To continue your hike, follow the trail to the left. You will find quite a few maidenhair and other ferns growing in this area. About 200 m later you will come to the second spur trail leading back to the overlook on the right. Continue straight ahead.

The trail threads its way along the hillside. There are no views through the deciduous trees here, but the mosses underfoot are nice and soft. You will cross a small ravine. Afterward the trail continues along a ridge, then bends back along the side of the ridge and starts to descend.

In a very short while the trail will merge with an old woods road. Continue straight ahead—do not turn back. The Slacks Trail ends at the White Rock Gap Trail, blazed orange. Again, the only trail sign, with an arrow pointing up, reads TORRY RIDGE TRAIL, giving the distance at 3.5 km (2.2 mi.).

WHITE ROCK GAP TRAIL

Length: 4 kilometers (2.5 miles)
Direction of travel: Southwest
Difficulty: Easy
Elevation: 595–778 meters (1,950–2,550 feet)
Difference in elevation: 183 meters (600 feet)
Markings: Orange blazes
Trail #: 480
How to get there: From Sherando take County Road 664 south to the Sherando Lake Campground. In the campground, follow the access road through to the upper lake. As the road turns up the hill toward the group camping area, you will see a grassy meadow beside the dam that forms the upper lake. The trail leaves from the far side of this meadow. The other end of the trail is between Mileposts 18 and 19 on the Blue Ridge Parkway.
Trail description: Cross the meadow beside the dam, and enter the forest via a woods road.

Shortly you will see the White Rock Gap Trail leaving the woods road to the right and starting up a hill. The road, which was an earlier route of the trail, follows the lakeside but eventually becomes overgrown. Follow the blazes for the White Rock Gap Trail, which passes over a rise and then runs parallel to the stream, which winds its way among big rocks, making it very picturesque.

The trail now follows another old road and quickly crosses a tributary creek. There is some flat space around here for a possible campsite. After passing a ravine the trail bends to the left and continues to follow the stream, usually about 20–50 m above it. You can hear it bubbling along but will rarely catch a glimpse of it. The trail itself is well maintained.

After about 1.6 km (1 mi.) the trail returns to the stream. You will find a beautiful campsite here, complete with a nice swimming hole. Shortly after this spot the trail crosses a small creek. Not far from here you will find the junction with the Slacks Trail. Watch the blazes and stay on the White Rock Gap Trail.

Quite a few trees have been killed in this area by gypsy moths. A sign beside the trail proclaims that here was an "old mountain homesite" dating back more than a century.

Now you come to the headwaters of the North Fork Back Creek, which supplies the water for Sherando Lake. (The Blue Ridge Parkway at White Rock Gap, between Mileposts 18 and 19, is just beyond.) From the Parkway it is 4 km (2.5 mi.) back to Sherando Lake and 0.5 km (0.3 mi.) to White Rock Gap.

WHITE ROCK FALLS TRAIL

Length: 4 kilometers (2.5 miles)
Direction of travel: Circuit, together with Slacks Trail
Difficulty: Moderate
Elevation: 702–851 meters (2,300–2,790 feet)
Difference in elevation: 149 meters (490 feet)
Markings: Yellow blazes
Trail #: None
How to get there: The trail starts just south of the Slacks Overlook, which is just after Milepost 19 on the Blue Ridge Parkway. The other end of the trail is at White Rock Gap, between Mileposts 18 and 19 on the parkway.
Trail description: There is a double yellow blaze on a tree at the trailhead. Enter the woods on a good trail, and start going downhill moderately. Almost immediately you will find many azaleas growing here, which are followed by rhododendron. Soon you will cross a creek on a log bridge.

Continue along the winding trail, and you will soon come to another stream. This one you will have to hop across on stones. Unless the water is high, there should be no problem negotiating the stream. On the other side, to the right, is a beautiful, level campsite among hemlocks and rhododendron. Watch carefully for the trail blazes if you have come from White Rock Gap—the turn across the creek is easy to miss.

The trail now makes a sharp left turn and continues going gently downhill not far from the creek. Rhododendron grow along the way and should look beautiful when in bloom, probably toward the end of June or early July. Where the rhododendron are not so thick, you may want to take a side trip to the creek bank. There are some beautiful spots with small cascades among the rocks.

The trail ascends gently to a rise. You are actually at the top of some cliffs, a few meters from the edge. If you go close to the edge, be careful you don't slip. The view is not particularly good along the hollow.

Now the trail descends from the cliff tops in a long switchback. Continue until you come to a sharp right downhill turn. The cliffs rise to your left. The spur trail to the falls continues straight ahead (the sign is on a tree to your left at the junction—it is easier to see if you come from White Rock Gap).

Following the spur trail straight ahead, go around the base of the cliffs. You will find yourself in a beautiful amphitheater, surrounded on three sides by vertical cliffs. Straight ahead are the White Rock Falls, where the waters of the creek tumble down several meters. It is cool and moist here, and the water is crystal clear.

Back at the junction of this spur trail with the main trail, turn right and go downhill steeply via switchbacks. A number of step falls can be seen or heard along the way. The trail now crosses the creek and continues with some ups and downs, then meets an old woods road and follows it for a bit. It soon leaves the road again, and now an old stone wall parallels the trail about 10 meters to the right.

The trail runs along a small creek with huge boulders in its bed. Then there are three footbridges that cross tiny creeks. Just after these you will arrive at the Blue Ridge Parkway. The trail sign there tells you it is 2.5 km (1.4 mi.) to the White Rock Falls, 4 km (2.5 mi.) to the Slacks Overlook, and 4.2 km (2.6 mi.) to the Torry Ridge Trail.

OREBANK CREEK ROAD

Length: 2.4 kilometers (1.5 miles)
Direction of travel: Southwest
Difficulty: Easy
Elevation: 488–549 meters (1,600–1,800 feet)
Difference in elevation: 61 meters (200 feet)
Markings: None needed
Trail #: None
How to get there: From Sherando take County Road 664 south and turn right onto Forest Development Road 42. At 0.8 km (0.5 mi.) from County Road 664, the Orebank Creek Road leaves to the left.
Trail description: The Orebank Creek Road is a jeep road which is open to traffic during most of the year, although it does have a gate. The road is passable for vehicles with high clearance.

Mostly level, this road ascends only slightly. If you walk or drive along here, you will quickly come to a side road on the right, which is gated. This spur, an old woods road, leads past some meadows with rows of autumn olive bushes. You can find some nice camping spots here, although you will have to bring your own water. After these clearings the road passes through the woods and ascends very gently. At one point the road divides: The right fork dead-ends at a campsite beside a stream, and the left fork is a continuation of the road. You will have to cross the stream (Mills Creek) shortly. Unless the water is very low, this will require wading. Continue through the woods until you arrive at the Reservoir Trail which, at this point, is still a road. Turning left here will bring you to the reservoir quickly.

After the spur branches off, the Orebank Creek Road, rising slowly, continues through the woods. The creek is not very close at this point, but the road gradually approaches it and meets it at the clearing where the Mills Creek Trail comes in from the left. This is the end of the Orebank Creek Road, which continues straight ahead over some berms as the Mills Creek Trail.

JEFFERSON
NATIONAL FOREST

7
James River Face Wilderness

The James River Face Wilderness consists of 35.6 square kilometers (8,800 acres) along the south bank of the James River, where the river breaks through the Blue Ridge Mountains. It is named for the cliffs and bluffs carved out of the 250 million-year-old Appalachian Mountains by the river. The James River Watergap is an excellent example of a geologic anticline. The area is composed of Precambrian and Paleozoic rock formations. Extensive uplifting and folding occurred in the formation of this section of the Blue Ridge Range.

The U.S. Forest Service administers this designated wilderness, whose most prominent features are its ruggedness and inaccessibility. All trails climb sharply during their ascent toward the central ridges. These steep grades make hiking strenuous. Only an occasional rumbling of a Norfolk and Western Railroad coal train, along the north bank of the James, disturbs the stillness.

Probably few, if any, settlers ever tried making a living in this region because of its unfriendly topography. At the beginning of this century, the land adjacent to the James River was logged. Nevertheless, little evidence of this cutting is visible today, and the old logging roads have become hiking trails. During the 1960s some commercial timbering took place, but evidence of that is hard to find.

Scars of mining operations, however, are slow to heal, and two remain visible: one along the north bank of the river near Little Rocky Row, the second within the designated wilderness itself, along Petites Gap Road. Activities at the latter site terminated long before the area was designated a wilderness.

Two hydroelectric dams have been located on the James River.

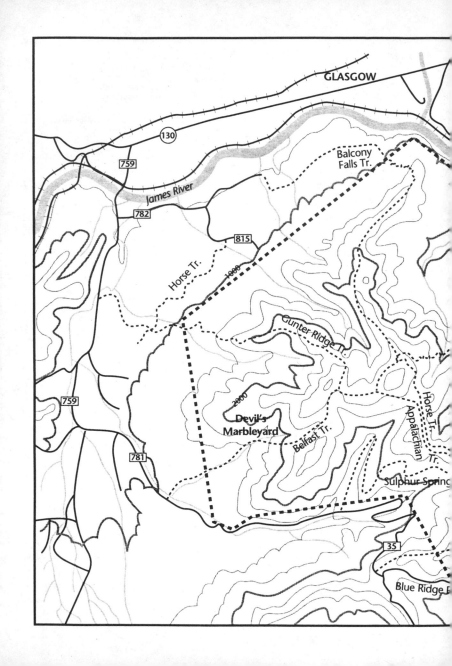

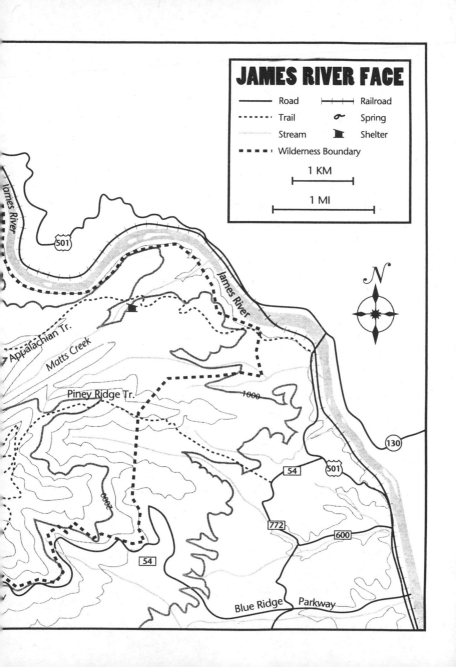

The dam at Balcony Falls was demolished in 1974 because it was no longer needed. The second, Snowden Dam, is situated just above the point where U.S. 501 crosses the river.

Old jeep trails in the James River Face Wilderness are no longer open to motorized vehicles. Certain designated paths may be open to horses, but it would be wise to check with the local ranger before bringing any animals there. Most trails are very steep, and no horses are allowed on the Appalachian Trail (AT), the Gunter Ridge, and the Belfast trails. There are trails around the perimeter of the area that lend themselves well to riding.

Chestnut oak, pitch pine, Virginia pine, table-mountain pine, yellow poplar, red and white oak, and hickory grow thickly. Along the Belfast and Gunter Ridge trails, particularly, galax covers the ground. Many of the large pines, especially along the Piney Ridge Trail, have been killed by pine bark beetles, which come in cycles.

The AT is the most hiked in the tract, and the immediate surroundings of its one shelter show signs of very heavy use. Avoid taking large groups into the Face, especially overnight, because flat camping sites are rare. Staying at the AT shelter may be a crowded affair if other hikers are using it the same night.

Car camping on the perimeter of the area is another alternative and likely to be more pleasant than staying at the often over-crowded shelter. The land at the perimeter is rather flat, and many camping spots are available. A Forest Service campground, Cave Mountain Lake, is nearby. From this campground all the trails except the AT at Route 501 and the Piney Ridge Trail are a short drive by car.

Try to plan your trip in the off-season rather than at a time when everybody goes hiking. You will enjoy your stay more if you do not encounter a steady stream of people along the trails. If you go during the winter, take warm clothes. It is cold in the Face and, if the wind is blowing too, it can be numbing! During the summer, long pants can be an advantage, as some trails wander through brier patches, nettles, and poison ivy.

Water is scarce on the ridges of which the Face largely consists.

If you're visiting the Face for one or two days, you can park your car along the side of a road or in an indentation in the forest at a trailhead without too much worry. But if you plan to extend your stay beyond that, it might be wise to arrange for the security of the car in other ways.

Maps: USGS Snowden quadrangle, 7.5 minute series; Glenwood Ranger District map, Jefferson National Forest.

APPALACHIAN TRAIL

Length: 16.9 kilometers (10.5 miles)
Direction of travel: North and east
Difficulty: Strenuous
Elevation: 722–937–219 meters (2,369–3,073–720 feet)
Difference in elevation: 215–718 meters (704–2,353 feet)
Markings: White blazes
Trail #: 1
How to get there: To hike the Appalachian Trail through the James River Face, you will need a car shuttle. From Glasgow take U.S. 501 southeast. Shortly after you cross the James River near Snowden Dam, you will see the white blazes for the AT turning off to the right. Park one car off the road, to pick up at the end of the hike. Continue on in the second car on U.S. 501 south to the Blue Ridge Parkway and turn south on it. Go to the Petites Gap exit and Forest Development Road 35 (County Road 781). You will see the AT's white blazes almost immediately. Park your car off the road and start up the trail on your right.
Trail description: Starting at Petites Gap on FDR 35, the AT climbs, at times very steeply, until it reaches Highcock Knob (937 m; 3,073 ft.). The trail leads through woods with large trees and without any particularly good views along this stretch.

We highly recommend long pants and maybe even a long-sleeved shirt when hiking this part of the trail in summer—waist-high nettles will keep your attention until a little past the top on the other side of Highcock Knob. The descent is at first very steep and then continues more moderately downhill via a long switchback.

At 3.8 km (2.4 mi.) there is a spring about 120 m from the trail. There is a good campsite here, on a flat saddle, the former site of Marble Spring Shelter.

Continuing 0.8 km (0.5 mi.) along the AT, ascending moderately through pleasant woods, you will come upon a junction from which several trails diverge. To your left the Sulphur Spring Trail goes downhill until it meets County Road 781 (FDR 35). To the right is a trail with a sign reading WATER HOLE ¼ MILE. This leads to a mudhole with water that is not fit for drinking even after treatment. A few steps farther, also to the right, a horse trail which was originally a fire road leaves from this junction. The Piney Ridge Trail branches right from the horse trail a few paces up the hill. The AT continues straight ahead and is marked by the usual white blazes.

The AT now bypasses peaks and follows steep hillsides, and in other places it travels over saddles and long ridges.

At 2.6 km (1.6 mi.) from the junction of the Sulphur Spring and Piney Ridge trails, the AT veers off to the left at an almost right angle. It climbs steeply along a hillside, where no good views through the thick deciduous woods are available. Another 0.6 km (0.4 mi.) farther brings you to the junction with the Belfast Trail. The AT again makes a sharp turn, this time to the right, while the Belfast Trail leaves to the left.

The AT then descends on the other side of the hill, crossing the old road again. At this point the Balcony Falls Trail runs off to the left and along the old road.

Follow the white blazes. Now the AT steeply descends the mountainside in a series of switchbacks. The view of the rapids of the James River and Snowden Dam below them and the bluffs dropping vertically down to the water are spectacular. Mountain laurel and rhododendron are abundant along the trail.

At the base of the switchbacks you will find a little stream with water. From here the trail passes along a steep hillside, alternately climbing and descending until it reaches the crest of a narrow

130

ridge. It follows along this ridge for a while with occasional views of the James River rapids, then falls off the ridge and descends the hillside at a constant but rather steep grade until 4 km (2.5 mi.) farther down the trail from the stream you reach Matts Creek Shelter. There are several good campsites around the shelter, but the area shows signs of heavy use. A creek flows close by.

Passing the shelter, the AT ascends, in parts steeply, the side of a mountain. It skirts a ridge, providing some good views of the James River, then drops and soon levels off for some distance. The final descent to U.S. 501, of approximately 1.3 km (0.8 mi.), is steep in places. The total distance from the Matts Creek Shelter to 501 is 4 km (2.5 mi.).

PINEY RIDGE TRAIL

Length: 5.6 kilometers (3.5 miles)
Direction of travel: West
Difficulty: Moderate to strenuous
Elevation: 280–756 meters (920–2,480 feet)
Difference in elevation: 476 meters (1,560 feet)
Markings: Blue blazes; trail infrequently used and somewhat obscure at times
Trail #: 2
How to get there: From Glasgow, take U.S. 501 southeast across the James River. Turn right on Forest Development Road 54 2.3 km (1.4 mi.) after crossing the river, just before the top of the hill. Watch the mileage carefully; the brown Forest Service sign is several feet away from Route 501 and very easy to miss. Just past a large hunting and fishing lodge, the road forks. (If the road is posted against trespassing before the lodge, ignore it—the sign is supposed to mark only the woods to the left of the road.) Take the right fork of the road and about 100 m later park in a large clearing. The trail starts as a continuation of this road.

You can reach the other end of the trail via the Appalachian Trail or the Sulphur Spring Trail.

Trail description: At first the trail is an old logging road leading through woods and closed to motorized vehicles.

After passing a closed gate, take the right-hand fork of the road. It climbs moderately for a short stretch and then, with a left turn, continues almost level.

The trail follows along the ridge top as an old woods road, in places grown over with pine and locust, and is pleasant to walk. There should be a good supply of blueberries in season. The rate of the climb increases somewhat.

The road gradually turns into a foot trail and starts a steep climb via several switchbacks. The trail is very narrow in places as it threads its way along the side of a steep slope. Nonetheless it is well constructed and easy to follow.

The hike now leads along a hillside ascending moderately. The large pines here have been killed off by pine bark beetles. You are looking down to the left into the narrow valley of Peters Creek. Climbing at a moderate rate, you pass a sign which marks the boundary of the wilderness area and then reach a small saddle.

For quite some distance after this, the trail runs along a steep hillside, bypassing two peaks along Piney Ridge, then descends very gradually, reaching a level section in a saddle. Here the trail again becomes an old woods road.

The hike through woods of pine, hemlock, and laurel along this section of the trail is very pleasant. The trees are beginning to reclaim the road and convert it into a footpath.

The trail climbs at a moderate rate up the ridge and then along the hillside. Just before the Piney Ridge Trail ends at the AT at 5.6 km (3.5 mi.), you will merge onto a woods road coming from the right that is designated as a horse trail. The AT is a few meters to the left along the horse trail. There is no sign at the junction with the horse trail, so if you are hiking this trail from the AT down, make sure you keep to the right after you have turned off the AT and onto the horse trail. A signpost does mark the trail junction at the intersection with the AT itself.

BELFAST TRAIL

Length: 4.8 kilometers (3 miles)
Direction of travel: East
Difficulty: Moderate to strenuous
Elevation: 305–808 meters (1,000–2,650 feet)
Difference in elevation: 503 meters (1,650 feet)
Markings: Intermittent blue blazes; trail generally easy to follow
Trail #: 9
How to get there: From Glasgow take Virginia Route 130 west to County Road 759. Go left on 759, crossing the James River, and drive 5 km (3.1 mi.) to County Road 781. Go left on 781 for 1.9 km (1.2 mi.) to the trail, on the left-hand side of the road. The trailhead is marked by a sign.

You can reach the other end of the trail via the Appalachian Trail.

Trail description: The Belfast Trail, at this point an old woods road, starts with a bridge across the East Fork of Elk Creek. At the far end of the bridge, you will find a sign telling you the closest trail junction—4 km (2.5 mi.) to the Gunter Ridge Trail and 4.8 km (3 mi.) to the AT. A few steps more and you will pass stone pillars announcing Camp Powhatan. This, apparently, was a summer camp once. It has fallen into ruin and not been used for quite some time.

Soon you will pass large concrete foundations, but any indication of what the buildings may have been have long since disappeared. A crossing of Belfast Creek is just ahead; it can be hopped across nicely on rocks.

The road forks several times. Stay on the main trail, leaving side trails that invite exploration for another day. Watch out for signs and blazes, and remain on the section that ascends gently but steadily. There are several possible campsites along the road.

For a while there are many pines along the trail. The trail climbs gently but steadily, then levels off for a short stretch. It crosses the creek and immediately crosses back again. The stream can be stepped over on stones.

The trail now begins to climb more steeply, passing through mostly deciduous woods. The higher you climb, the steeper the trail gets. It is also rather rocky at times, so watch your footing throughout.

At a little more than the halfway point of the trail, you will arrive at Devil's Marbleyard, a big rock slide. These sedimentary rocks were once part of the shoreline of an inland sea about 600 million years or so ago, during the Precambrian era. The rocks were uplifted and folded so hard, they cracked and spilled down the mountain.

At the lower end of the rock slide you will pass, on your right, a pretty waterfall down a vertical rock wall. When we first hiked the trail in midwinter, the fall was frozen into many big icicles and looked spectacular. In midsummer, though, this waterfall becomes just a trickle or may even dry up altogether.

Climbing very steeply, the trail skirts the foot of the rock slide. An obscure little path branches off to the left, leading to the slide itself and a view, if you get to the top.

After this very steep stretch, the Belfast Trail returns to a more gradual but still rather steep climb alongside the stream. There are a few smaller rock slides to the left of the trail, but they are nothing much to speak of.

The trail heads around to the top of a ravine, where there is a beautiful winter view of a deep valley. The trees roundabout are mostly deciduous and block the view when the leaves are out.

The trail again starts a steep climb to a saddle where the Gunter Ridge Trail terminates on the left (4 km; 2.5 mi.).

The Belfast Trail runs straight ahead and continues to climb moderately for a short stretch. It then descends slightly to end at the Appalachian Trail at 4.8 km (3 mi.).

GUNTER RIDGE TRAIL

Length: 7.2 kilometers (4.5 miles)
Direction of travel: East
Difficulty: Moderate to strenuous
Elevation: 244–768 meters (800–2,517 feet)
Difference in elevation: 524 meters (1,717 feet)
Markings: Blue blazes
Trail #: 8

How to get there: From Glasgow take Virginia Route 130 west to County Road 759. Go left for 2.4 km (1.5 mi.) on 759 to the trailhead, which is marked by a sign.

An alternate approach, which does not lead through private land and which has good parking facilities, is along a horse trail which crosses the Gunter Ridge Trail about 300 m after the latter enters the woods. On County Road 759 cross the James River and then turn left on County Road 782. Turn right on County Road 815 and follow the paved part of the road until you enter the forest. The road will turn to gravel. On the right you will soon see a gated road marked as a horse trail. This is the path you want to take. Follow the gravel road a little farther, and on the right you will find a large parking lot for horse trailers. Park your car(s) in a corner, leaving space for horse trailers.

The other end of the trail can be reached via the Belfast Trail.

Trail description: Starting on the left side of County Road 759, the Gunter Ridge Trail first follows a paved road. Follow this road straight in along a fence and take a right turn at the toolshed.

A little farther along, shortly after the trail enters the woods, there is another fork in the road. This time, take the left branch (the right branch leads to private land and is posted against trespassing), immediately crossing a small stream. Turn right, following the road around a very large berm until it joins again with the path that was blocked off. (Or if you like, scramble over the berm to rejoin the road on the other side.) The road passes through a wooded area containing beech, hemlock, pine, dogwood, hickory, and oak trees.

You will arrive shortly at a gravel road that crosses the trail here. This is a horse trail and is the alternate approach, described above, to the Gunter Ridge Trail. To use this approach, follow the gated road through woods to a stream with a concrete slab across. The crossing presents no problem in dry weather but could require wading after heavy rains or when the snow melts in spring. A little farther is a clearing—a small logging operation; take the main trail to the right into the woods. The trail is generally level with only a minor up and down. Ascend gently until you come to a large area with small trees on the right. Continue following the road and in a short while, at the end of the clearing, you will cross Little Hellgate Creek, which probably runs most of the year. A few meters around the next bend and you will already see the sign for the Gunter Ridge Trail. Turn left and uphill here.

At first the Gunter Ridge Trail ascends gently through the woods. Soon after entering the wilderness area, you will have to cross Little Hellgate Creek.

Now hemlocks are getting sparse, and mountain laurel take their place. You will find some galax, with its shiny red and green leaves, along the trail.

The Gunter Ridge Trail now begins to climb noticeably, leaving the stream in the ravine below to the right. Switchbacks start shortly after this, some eighteen of them. Along the way, you will see a few good spots for viewing the valley below and your starting point, especially in winter. The trees roundabout are mostly deciduous.

The trail continues to climb up the ridge and passes slightly to the right of a knob. After a short dip, it follows the ridge. It then skirts a second knob, leaving it to the left, and passes over a slight saddle. This is a spot for a campsite if you carry your water. The trail then continues slightly uphill to end at the Belfast Trail at 7.2

km (4.5 mi.). To the left it is 0.8 km (0.5 mi.) to the AT, to the right 4 km (2.5 mi.) to County Road 759.

BALCONY FALLS TRAIL

Length: 8 kilometers (5 miles)
Direction of travel: East and south
Difficulty: Moderate to strenuous
Elevation: 229–789 meters (750–2,588 feet)
Difference in elevation: 560 meters (1,838 feet)
Markings: Blue blazes
Trail #: 7
How to get there: From Glasgow take Virginia Route 130 west to County Road 759. Go left on 759, crossing the James River, and then turn left on County Road 782. Go to the end of the road and park in the "Locher Tract" parking lot. The trail starts at the far end of the parking lot. Go through the stile and follow the grassy center path until it joins the dirt road. Alternatively, climb over the gate blocking the continuation of the road through the parking lot and walk a short stretch along it until you see the grassy path coming in from the left. Continue along the dirt road, and shortly after crossing a small stream you will see the trail going into the woods on the right.

The other end of the trail can be reached via the Appalachian Trail.

Trail description: The trail starts out as a foot trail, running beside the stream through lush lowland forest. In a few hundred meters, it encounters an old woods road and turns left, leaving the stream. A sign marks the intersection.

With only minor ups and downs, the road continues for 2.4 km (1.5 mi.). Close to the place where it turns into a foot trail, you will cross a streambed with water, though it may dry up in late summer and fall. After this, there is no other water along the trail. A sign indicates the wilderness boundary.

At this point the trail begins to climb steeply via innumerable switchbacks—we counted about twenty-two of them. The vegetation consists largely of pines and laurel.

The trail now continues, climbing along a narrow ridge for a short stretch, then leveling off. At several points the trail drops off the ridge top to bypass rocky outcrops, then turns via a single switchback to regain or cross it. Then the trail climbs moderately up through deciduous woods.

At 5.6 km (3.5 mi.) the trail turns into an old woods road. You will find a Forest Service sign here supplying various distances: Locher Tract 6.5 km (4 mi.), AT 2.4 km (1.5 mi.), Petites Gap Road 10.4 km (6.5 mi.).

The road ascends gently, for the most part, through very rocky pine woods. On your right you will see a stone slide in Sawmill Hollow. A deep ravine, also on your right, follows. Rocky pine woods continue on both sides of the trail.

After a sharp left turn immediately before the ridge top, the Balcony Falls Trail ends at the AT. A sign at the trail junction furnishes distances to different points: Locher Tract 8 km (5 mi.), Matts Creek Shelter 4.5 km (2.8 mi.).

SULPHUR SPRING TRAIL

Length: 4.8 kilometers (3 miles)
Direction of travel: Generally east
Difficulty: Moderate
Elevation: 442–747 meters (1,450–2,450 feet)
Difference in elevation: 305 meters (1,000 feet)
Markings: None
Trail #: 3001
How to get there: From Glasgow take U.S. 501 south to the Blue Ridge Parkway and turn south on it. Go to the Petites Gap exit and Forest Development Road 35 (County Road 781). Go past the white blazes of the Appalachian Trail and continue downhill in

some long switchbacks. Shortly afterward you will come to a small bridge across a creek and the trailhead on the right. There are two boulders and a trail sign. Parking space is enough for two or three cars.

The other end of the trail can be reached via the AT or the Piney Ridge Trail.

Trail description: The Sulphur Spring Trail starts as an old road with a stream on the right.

After about 50 m you will encounter a trail register. This is a "foot and horse trail" although there is no mention of it on the register. Two thirds of the way up, this trail becomes weedy and rather overgrown in summer and may be difficult for horses.

The trail leaves the creek after 200 m and leads through many weeds, much of it poison ivy. Eventually the trail rejoins the stream and then crosses it. The creek, only 1 or 2 meters wide, can be easily negotiated.

The trail now starts to climb more noticeably. There are some nice views of Thunder Ridge to the south and of the length of Petites Gap in winter; in summer most of these views can only be guessed through the foliage.

Some maintenance has been done, but the brush and weeds eventually become waist high in places. This generally poses no problem to the hiker although you may consider wearing long pants as there are several more patches of poison ivy. There are two views through gaps in the trees when you pass through some of these weedy spots.

The trail continues to ascend, hugging the side of the ridge. You can walk around the many small pines growing in and along the trail.

After a while you will come to a rock wall on your left. It is about 6 m high. If you climb up, you will be rewarded with a great view. If you don't feel like making the scramble, turn right and step out onto some rocky outcrops opposite the wall and enjoy the same neat view on easier terms. You will also find some wild bleeding hearts growing here.

Soon afterward you will reach the junction with the AT. Going north from here it is 8.2 km (5.1 mi.) to Matts Creek Shelter, 12.4 km (7.7 mi.) to Snowden Bridge. To the south it is about 0.8 km (0.5 mi.) to Marble Springs and 4.3 km (2.7 mi.) to Petites Gap along the AT. Diagonally across you will find the Piney Ridge Trail, which is 5.6 km (3.5 mi.) to FDR 54.

The horse trail which leads to the Piney Ridge Trail originally was an old fire road. It still continues along the ridge of the mountain, relatively level with only minor ups and downs. It skirts several ridge tops until it meets the AT again at the junction with the Balcony Falls Trail. The Forest Service calls this section a continuation of the Sulphur Spring Trail, though it seems to be little used.

8
Mountain Lake Wilderness

The Mountain Lake area is a high massif situated northwest of the town of Blacksburg in Virginia's Giles and Craig counties and West Virginia's Monroe County. The Mountain Lake Wilderness measures 43.5 square kilometers (10,700 acres).

Before the U.S. Forest Service acquired the land in the early part of this century, it had been largely cut over. As a result, most of the stands in the forest are roughly of even age. The Forest Service has logged only a little more than 0.4 square kilometers (100 acres), and the forest is beginning to mature.

Mountain Lake is one of only two natural lakes in Virginia, the other being Lake Drummond in the Dismal Swamp near Norfolk. The lake was first noted by a survey party in 1751. At that time raiding parties of Indians still roamed Virginia. During the Civil War, the Salt Sulphur Turnpike—now County Roads 700 and 613—was used to transport troops and matériel across the mountain. When Union forces retreated in 1864, they discarded ammunition and other heavy items at a place now known as Minie Ball Hill, where some of them may still be found. (Minie balls were bullets used in the nineteenth century.) You can also find arrowheads throughout the Mountain Lake area.

Mountain Lake itself and some of the surrounding area is private property and belongs to the Mountain Lake Hotel. The view from the main structure over the lake is beautiful. The hotel itself is a nice, albeit somewhat expensive, alternative to camping. Be warned though that your "bush clothes" are not acceptable during dinner hour.

In 1960 the Forest Service created a 6.1 square kilometer (1,500 acre) scenic area comprising Wind Rock, Lone Pine Peak, War Spur

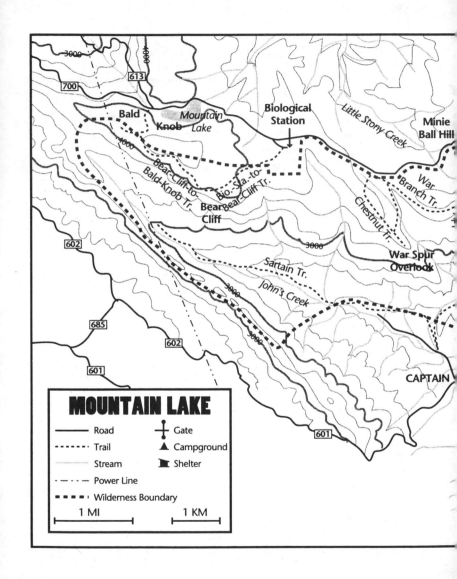

MOUNTAIN LAKE

—— Road	┼ Gate
---- Trail	▲ Campground
∼∼∼ Stream	🛏 Shelter
—·—· Power Line	
▬▬▬ Wilderness Boundary	

1 MI   1 KM

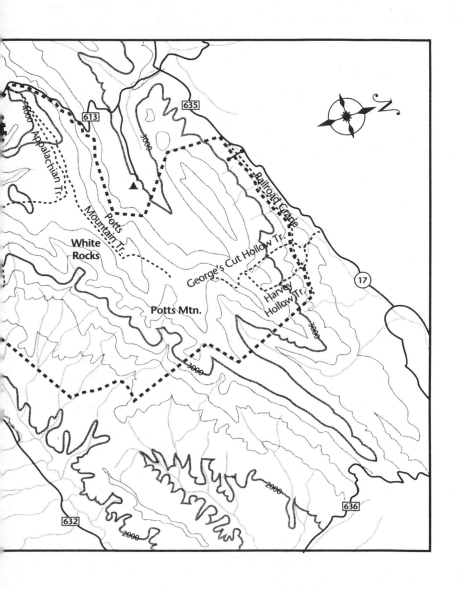

Branch with its virgin trees, and War Spur Overlook. The Mountain Lake Wilderness was established in 1984 and increased to a total size of 43.5 square kilometers (10,700 acres) in 1988.

There are three forest zones in the Mountain Lake region. The Canadian Zone—generally above 1,220 meters (4,000 feet)—has red spruce, hemlock, yellow birch, and many other trees that are found mostly on high southern peaks. The forest around the edge of Mountain Lake itself reflects this zone, but the lake and its drainage basin are not part of the wilderness.

The Transition Zone—between 760 and 1,220 meters (2,500 and 4,000 feet)—predominates because most of the land lies in this altitude range. Various oaks, as well as hickories, walnuts, yellow poplars, Virginia and table-mountain pine, and other less common species occur throughout the Transition Zone. American chestnuts were once plentiful.

In the Upper Austral or Upper Carolinian Zone—generally 760 meters (2,500 feet) and below—grow various kinds of pine and oak, maples, eastern redbud, black walnuts, sassafras, locusts, cherries, and many more. You will find this vegetation mostly along John's Creek drainage. This zone shares much of the same flora with the Piedmont Zone of central Virginia.

More than nine hundred kinds of flowering plants have been identified in the scenic area alone. Rhododendron are plentiful throughout the region, forming dense stands in several places. Mountain laurel and flame azaleas add charm and grace to the woods and make tough going for the bushwhacker. Greenbrier, raspberries, blackberries, and—at lower elevations—poison ivy are common. Many mushrooms and fungi, poisonous as well as edible, can be found. The height of the mushroom season is late July through August. Use extreme caution in identifying and eating mushrooms—in fact, abstain altogether unless you are a true expert in this field.

Timber rattlesnakes, copperheads, and black snakes (the last, nonvenomous) are fairly common in the Mountain Lake area. Among the nine or ten species of salamander found, the red-backed salamander is most prevalent. According to biologists at the University of Virginia's Mountain Lake Biological Station, more than one hundred species of birds have been recorded. You can find native brook trout in Little Stony Creek, John's Creek, War Branch, and White Rock Branch.

The eastern continental divide coincides with the ridge tops of Salt Pond Mountain, Potts Mountain, and John's Creek Mountain. Rain falling into the John's Creek drainage flows into the Atlantic Ocean, and water running into Little Stony Creek and White Rock Branch flows into the Gulf of Mexico.

At Bald Knob and Bear Cliff there are some outcrops of sandstone bedrock, deposited as sediment about 400 million years ago during the Silurian period. Outcrops at War Spur Overlook, Wind Rock, and White Rocks are probably of similar age and origin.

The climate is characterized by marked changes in weather. Annual precipitation exceeds 100 centimeters (40 inches). The temperature ranges from a record low of minus 32 degrees Celsius (minus 26 degrees Fahrenheit) to a maximum of approximately 29 degrees Celsius (85 degrees Fahrenheit). Summer thunderstorms are frequent, so go prepared with rain gear.

There are a number of good camping spots in the area, but water may be a problem at high elevations. The Forest Service's Wind Rock Campground is located off Route 613 on the north side of the mountain. If you plan to do any hiking along trails that are overgrown and hard to follow, take along topographic maps and a compass, especially if you will be bushwhacking.

No camping or fire permits are necessary at this time.

Maps: USGS Interior, Waiteville, Eggleston, and Newport quadrangles, 7.5 minute series.

BIOLOGICAL STATION–BEAR CLIFF TRAIL

Length: 1.4 kilometers (0.9 mile)
Direction of travel: South
Difficulty: Easy
Elevation: 1,165–1,250 meters (3,820–4,100 feet)
Difference in elevation: 85 meters (280 feet)
Markings: None at first, later yellow blazes
Trail #: None

How to get there: Take U.S. 460 west from Blacksburg, past Newport, to the junction with County Road 700. Turn right and follow 700—which becomes 613 beyond the Mountain Lake Hotel. Go past the hotel to the Mountain Lake Biological Station. This trail, as well as the trail system behind the Biological Station, is subject to private property rights and should not be used without permission. Go to the office or see the caretaker of the station in the off-season. When the station is open, park in the station's parking lot near the office and walk back to the trailhead. In the off-season, park along the road, taking care that you do not block any gates or roads.

The other end of the trail is reached via the Bear-Cliff-to-Bald-Knob Trail.

Trail description: At the entrance of the biological station grounds, the road forks. On your right will be a metal gate next to a tree with a NO TRESPASSING sign. Go through the gate and up the narrow road 0.8 km (0.5 mi.) to a small wire-fence springhouse. A somewhat indistinct foot trail with frequent, but sometimes faint, yellow blazes continues on around the right side of the springhouse and gently winds uphill through mixed deciduous forest.

DO NOT wander from the road/trail or disturb anything along it, no matter how intriguing. The equipment along the trail belongs to the biological station and is part of ongoing scientific investigations. Tampering with the equipment may result in revocation of access privileges.

In a little while you will arrive at a short, steeper stretch, which takes you up to the broad ridge of Salt Pond Mountain.

Bear Cliff is located 0.5 km (0.3 mi.) across the crest, just past the point where the trail starts to descend the other side. A sign marks the intersection with the trail to Bald Knob. Continue straight ahead to Bear Cliffs, which is a descending series of four or five sandstone tiers, each about 30 m long, 6 to 12 m high, and separated from each other by a space of 3 to 5 m. The highest rock face measures no more than 18 m, but there are some interesting boulder problems for rock climbers.

The views to the east and south are quite beautiful and well worth the hike. On a clear day you can see the Peaks of Otter, northeast of Roanoke, and parts of Blacksburg, Christiansburg, and Radford, Virginia.

BEAR CLIFF–BALD KNOB TRAIL

Length: 3.7 kilometers (2.3 miles)
Direction of travel: Southwest
Difficulty: Moderate
Elevation: 1,251–1,324 meters (4,100–4,340 feet)
Difference in elevation: 73 meters (240 feet)
Markings: None; trail may be difficult to follow. Carry map and compass.
Trail #: None
How to get there: Via the Biological-Station-to-Bear-Cliff Trail, having received permission to hike it from the caretaker at the biological station.

To reach the other end of the trail, drive west from Blacksburg on U.S. 460, past Newport, until you arrive at the junction with County Road 700. Turn right and follow 700 to the Mountain Lake Hotel. Park there.

Hiking this trail in either direction requires permission from the Mountain Lake Hotel caretaker because it is subject to private property rights.

Trail description: Start your hike at the trail junction with the

Bear Cliffs Trail and follow it through a typical southern thicket with lots of mountain laurel. Brief glimpses of the Bald Knob microwave relay station are visible from some places in the thicket.

The trail may be difficult to follow at times, so watch for some blazes, cairns, or similar markings to stay on course; often it may seem not much more than a deer trail. Stay on the crest of the ridge and continue heading southwest.

Just inside the property boundary of the hotel, the trail forks. The right branch descends to the lake and trails on the hotel grounds. The left branch continues on toward Bald Knob.

At 2.1 km (1.3 mi.) from Bear Cliff you should meet a service road coming up Bald Knob from the Mountain Lake Hotel. Follow this road for 0.5 km (0.3 mi.) to the top of the mountain. Bald Knob is the highest point for many miles around, and the view is great.

You can walk back down the service road to the hotel and County Road 700.

CHESTNUT TRAIL–WAR SPUR OVERLOOK–
WAR BRANCH TRAIL–APPALACHIAN TRAIL

Length: 4 kilometers (2.5 miles)
Direction of travel: Circuit
Difficulty: Easy
Elevation: 1,153–1,068 meters (3,780–3,500 feet)
Difference in elevation: 85 meters (280 feet)
Markings: Sign with trail diagram at trailhead; trail easy to follow
Trail #: None
How to get there: From Blacksburg take U.S. 460 west, past the town of Newport, until the junction with County Road 700. Turn right and follow 700, or 613, as it is later numbered. Go past the Mountain Lake Hotel and the Mountain Lake Biological Station. About 2.6 km (1.6 mi.) later, look for a small parking lot on the right side of the road. The trail sign reads MOUNTAIN LAKE SCENIC AREA HIKING TRAILS. Park your car there.

Trail description: This is a nice circuit hike with a pretty view. Go right (south) at the sign onto the Chestnut Trail, crossing a small footbridge. The trail rises gently along War Spur to its rather broad crest.

The trail threads its way through mixed deciduous forest to the side trail leading to War Spur Overlook. From the trail junction it is 0.3 km (0.2 mi.) downhill to the overlook.

The overlook is a rock outcrop, which provides a nice view of a stand of virgin trees along War Branch. Retrace your steps along the Overlook Trail to the point where you left the Chestnut Trail to continue the circuit.

Back on the main trail, you pass through a couple of switchbacks, then go downhill through a rhododendron archway to the virgin forest. There you will encounter War Branch and enjoy the beauty of the old majestic trees. The stream drains from an area of heavy human use, so in spite of its pristine appearance, do not drink from it.

Cross the stream and follow the Chestnut Trail out of War Branch Hollow. The trail now leads through teaberry country.

At 3.5 km (2.2 mi.) you will arrive at the War Spur Connector with the Appalachian Trail. If you turn left at this T-junction, you will be back at the parking lot in 0.5 km (0.3 mi.).

If you wish to go to the AT, turn right at the T-junction. For 1.6 km (1 mi.) you will walk along a wide grassy path. On the lower slopes to your right is a virgin stand of hemlocks. Then the path descends about 60 m and joins the AT in a bend.

APPALACHIAN TRAIL

Length: 7.2 kilometers (4.5 miles)
Direction of travel: Generally east and south
Difficulty: Strenuous
Elevation: 1,259–616 meters (4,128–2,020 feet)
Difference in elevation: 643 meters (2,108 feet)

Markings: White blazes

Trail #: 1

How to get there: Take U.S. 460 west from Blacksburg, past Newport, until you arrive at the junction with County Road 700. Turn right and follow 700 (it becomes 613 after passing the Mountain Lake Hotel). Go past the Mountain Lake Hotel and the Mountain Lake Biological Station. Pass the trail sign reading MOUNTAIN LAKE SCENIC AREA HIKING TRAILS. The road may be rough in places. Watch for the spot, about 6 km (3.7 mi.) later, where the Appalachian Trail crosses the road on the ridge of Potts Mountain just before the road starts a steep descent on the other side.

To reach the other end, take U.S. 460 west from Blacksburg and turn north on Virginia Route 42 at Newport. After 0.8 km (0.5 mi.) turn left on County Road 601. Follow 601 through Clover Hollow to the small community of Captain. There turn left onto County Road 632. There is a small parking area to the right about 2.4 km (1.5 mi.) from Captain. Park here as the road becomes private property shortly after this. The trailhead is a few feet down the road on the right.

Trail description: The AT continues on the right side of the road on the ridge of Potts Mountain and goes gently uphill. You can walk along the old jeep road, now closed off with berms. The actual trail itself is located just to the right of the road, but rejoins it after the berms.

At 0.5 km (0.3 mi.) you will pass Wind Rock, which is located 30 m to the left of the trail near a small clearing. The rock offers a dramatic view to the northwest on clear days. To the left, you can see Peters Mountain on the other side of Stony Creek valley, as well as several other distant ridges.

At the clearing, which is a popular campsite, you will find two trails. The one going straight ahead is the Potts Mountain Trail, the one to the right is the rerouted AT, marked by white blazes.

The AT runs gently downhill along the side of the hill through scrubby woods. You may glimpse some meadows uphill to the left—the Potts Mountain Trail runs through these.

After approximately 1.6 km (1 mi.) you will find a grassy trail going off to the right and downhill. Follow the white blazes of the AT which continue straight ahead.

When the AT sharply curves to the right and starts going downhill, you will find the old junction with the Potts Mountain Trail. By following this overgrown path to the left, you will reach the trail along the ridge of Potts Mountain in a very short while. Turning left here will bring you back to the junction near Wind Rock.

After a brief descent on the AT, you will reach a broad saddle and for a while the AT follows it at a perfectly level grade, then starts its ascent to Lone Pine Peak through a beautiful carpet of ferns. The trail now starts a 610 m (2,000 ft.) descent to the floor of John's Creek valley. The trail is very narrow here until it encounters the War Branch Trail coming in from the right at 4.2 km (2.6 mi.), after descending for 120 m. The AT bends slightly left (east) here and continues steeply downhill, but is now wider.

About halfway down the hill you will have a good view over John's Creek valley. The forest changes subtly as you descend.

Below this viewpoint the AT becomes very steep, indeed, and in places is severely eroded. The Forest Service is planning to reroute this section of the AT into a series of switchbacks, beginning trail construction in the summer of 1994. As this project is likely to take several years, expect having to face this descent.

War Spur Shelter appears suddenly on the left as you reach the foot of Salt Pond Mountain. This is the end of this terribly steep part. War Spur Branch flows close by, lined by dense thickets of rhododendron.

Many mushrooms grow in this area in August. Don't eat any unless you know your mushrooms perfectly!

At War Spur Shelter the AT turns sharply right—the trail straight ahead leads to private land. There is a rough log bridge across War Spur Branch. The trail descends moderately after the section above the shelter, leaving the Wilderness area. In 1 km (0.6 mi.) you will reach County Road 632 in John's Creek valley.

POTTS MOUNTAIN TRAIL

Length: 8 kilometers (5 miles)
Direction of travel: Generally northeast
Difficulty: Moderate
Elevation: 1,240–897 meters (4,065–2,942 feet)
Difference in elevation: 343 meters (1,123 feet)
Markings: None
Trail #: 55

How to get there: Via the Appalachian Trail. Follow it for 0.5 km (0.3 mi.) to the junction at Wind Rock, where there is a clearing. At this spot the AT turns right; the Potts Mountain Trail begins here and runs straight ahead along the ridge of Potts Mountain.

Trail description: The Potts Mountain Trail is a pleasant walk along the ridge of the mountain through open woods with a dense grassy understory. It is really an old jeep and fire road, which has fallen somewhat into disrepair in the past, but according to the Forest Service it has now been adopted by a local riding club, so you may encounter horses on the trail.

A little farther along the trail is the site of the old Stony Creek fire tower. The tower has been dismantled and removed, and all that remains are five concrete support blocks. The trail now threads its way through a clearing, which gives a limited view to the east.

At 2.4 km (1.5 mi.) you will arrive at the former junction with the AT, which runs downhill just a few yards. A large white oak grows in the middle of the Potts Mountain Trail at this point, but there are no markings to indicate this junction, and it is very difficult to find from the Potts Mountain Trail. If you wish to make this a circuit hike, start along the AT at Wind Rock.

At 3.5 km (2.2 mi.) from its beginning, the Potts Mountain Trail arrives at White Rocks in a high saddle of Potts Mountain, near the spot where Virginia's Giles and Craig counties meet West Virginia's Monroe County. The White Rocks are leaning slabs of bedrock with a view of John's Creek valley to the south. The view is not overwhelming but the rocks are fun to scramble around in—with care. The Potts Mountain Trail provides the only access to these rocks.

Continuing along Potts Mountain Trail you will come to a number of rocky outcrops, none of which offers a view. But they do offer nice lunch sites.

Near these rocks the path leads through some clearings which, in July, are covered with mountain bugbane (*Cimicifuga americana*), a tall stalk with pretty white flowers. Another wildflower you can readily identify is the fire pink, a starlike red flower with five distinct petals.

Not far beyond these clearings, the trail petered out in an area of many downed trees and lots of brush when we were there. The Forest Service may have come in and done some clearing, but in any case the trail will soon come to the eastern boundary of the wilderness area. The private land beyond it is posted, as the owners do not wish horses and people on their property. There may eventually be a rerouting of the trail to the south, but not in the immediate future. So you should turn back here and retrace your steps.

SARTAIN TRAIL

Length: 4.8 kilometers (3 miles)
Direction of travel: Southwest
Difficulty: Moderate
Elevation: 641–915 meters (2,100–3,000 feet)
Difference in elevation: 274 meters (900 feet)
Markings: Yellow blazes
Trail #: None
How to get there: Take U.S. 460 west from Blacksburg and turn north on Virginia Route 42 at Newport. After 0.8 km (0.5 mi.) turn left on County Road 601. Follow 601 through Clover Hollow to the small community of Captain. There turn left onto County Road 632. Park your car before you reach the boundary of the Mountain Lake Wilderness, 2.4 km (1.5 mi.) from Captain.

You will have to retrace your steps on this trail, as there is no connecting trail to use for a circuit hike.

Trail description: The Sartain Trail starts as a "Wilderness Access Trail" a few feet beyond the junction with the Appalachian Trail on County Road 632. At first it is an old woods road that runs along the side of a grassy clearing. This clearing, first glimpsed through the trees, is private property. The trees along the left side of the trail are marked with red blazes, indicating the boundary. Watch the blazes carefully—soon the woods road turns left and into the private property, and you will have to follow the newly blazed trees straight ahead. A faint trail to the right will lead you to the AT.

After the trail leaves the old woods road, it continues skirting privately owned land for about 1.6 km (1 mi.). The hike along a barbed wire fence—to keep you from trespassing—and the steep dips across the trail should be eliminated by the rerouting of the trail higher up on the hillside, which was planned by the Forest Service for the summer of 1993. Afterward the trail again becomes an old woods road.

Shortly thereafter you will come to a T-end with a double blazed tree. The Sartain Trail turns left here along another old woods road, then joins yet a third. This third road leads to the private property you skirted earlier and is gated. Turn right.

Now the Sartain Trail becomes a pleasant hike along a stream valley. The cleared land ends just about where the trail first enters the wilderness area, and the rest of the walk is largely through woods, with some understory of mountain laurel and rhododendron. Some of the best hunting and fishing in the region is found in this valley.

As you walk along, the trail climbs a little, but it never becomes very steep. You will pass several tributaries, but crossing them should present no problem. Neither should walking around downed trees.

There are some nice camping spots in the area, but you will have to backpack as there is no access for car camping. The Sartain Trail itself hugs the wilderness area for a while but never enters it for long. The reason for this is a long, narrow inholding along the creek.

The trail ends high in John's Creek valley at a power line and right-of-way (4.8 km; 3 mi.). Here you will have to turn back and retrace your steps, unless you are a confirmed bushwhacker and have maps and compass along. Then you can either follow the creek to its source or even try to reach the summit of Bald Knob.

GEORGE'S CUT HOLLOW AND HARVEY HOLLOW TRAILS

Length: 6.2 kilometers (3.9 miles)
Direction of travel: Generally south
Difficulty: Moderate
Elevation: 732–1,006 meters (2,400–3,300 feet)
Difference in elevation: 274 meters (900 feet)
Markings: None; trailheads somewhat obscure
Trail #: None
How to get there: From Blacksburg, take U.S. 460 west, past Newport and Pembroke. Before you get to the bridge over the New River, turn right (north) on County Road 635. Continue on this road past the APG Lime plant and the signs for the White Rocks campground. Soon you will see a sign indicating that you are entering Monroe County, West Virginia. The road now becomes West Virginia Route 17, and the trails start 3.2 km (2 mi.) after this sign, at a point where a wide shoulder on the road allows a good parking spot. No sign is present, but an accumulation of beer cans is. The trail plunges down the embankment and into the woods. If you pass a house set back a bit from the road on the left, you have gone too far. There is a very obscure national forest sign just before you come to the house, also on the left.

An alternate approach is along a gated road, Forest Development Road 10531, which starts from West Virginia Route 17 about 0.3 km (0.2 mi.) after entering Monroe County.

Trail description: Going down the bank of the road through some weeds, you will find a faint trail. You may recognize it by the litter along its beginning. Follow this trail through a rhododendron thicket to a stream. You can easily hop across. Stepping up a steep bank, follow the trail until you hit an old woods road. Turn right here. This junction is fairly obscure, so you may want to mark it inconspicuously for your return.

The trail follows this old road gently uphill. Ignore a survey line intersecting along the way. Continue following the road until you come to a fork—one trail goes straight ahead through a rhododendron thicket and across another stream, the other turns left and uphill. This is where the George's Cut Hollow Trail (straight ahead) and the Harvey Hollow Trail (left) part company.

Take the Harvey Hollow Trail uphill. There are a number of small pines growing in the trail at the fork, but not for long. The trail climbs more noticeably than the old woods road, but not very steeply yet. There are many rhododendron and hemlocks along the trail.

In about 0.5 km (0.3 mi.) the trail peters out, and you are confronted with a steep, but not very high, hillside. If you look to the left you will find a very faint trail going up to what looks like a small saddle. Follow this and you will reach the top, where there is a level, grassy old railroad grade. Many spicebushes grow here.

Turn right along the grade and go a hundred or so meters along it until you have passed the hollow and you see a hillside rising on your left. An old woods road turns left here. This is the continuation of the Harvey Hollow Trail.

The Mountain Lake Wilderness boundary runs along this old railroad grade, which is actually an alternate approach to these trails. If you follow it you will first come to the crossing of the George's Cut Hollow Trail. Going through some wet spots and alternately passing steep hillsides and hollows on your left, sometimes with dense rhododendron thickets, it continues absolutely level until it reaches a gate at West Virginia Route 17.

After a brief dip, the Harvey Hollow Trail starts climbing

steadily, at times steeply, but never leveling for more than a few meters. On the left the stream flows close by, but it is intermittent and it would be wise not to rely on it for water. Many rhododendron and hemlocks grow on both sides of the streambed, while the woods to the right of the trail are open for a while.

As the hollow narrows, the old road becomes steeper and more overgrown with small trees. You may also find a lot of downed timber across the trail. The Forest Service at present does not maintain these trails, which are still pleasant and relatively easy to follow. At times a lot of ferns grow in the roadbed.

Continue following the old road. The climb becomes more gentle and eventually you will top the rise, pass behind a knob, and start to descend. In a level spot you will suddenly come upon an obscure trail junction. Here the Harvey Hollow Trail meets the George's Cut Hollow Trail and dead-ends.

Turning left, the George's Cut Hollow Trail climbs the mountain, rising another 122 m above the trail junction before you have to turn back. It first climbs along a hillside and then, turning back on itself, follows an almost level ridge. Although overgrown with ferns and frequently blocked by fallen trees, the trail is pleasant, but it peters out about 1.4 km (0.9 mi.) from the junction.

To follow the George's Cut Hollow Trail downhill, go straight ahead through a bunch of small trees and brush growing in the junction. Once past these, the trail becomes fairly clear again.

To the right, just after the junction, are some nice big rocks that make a perfect lunch spot, although the deciduous trees around them are all too tall to permit you any view, at least in summer.

Right near these rocks the trail seems to divide—stay on the part that runs right in the creek bed—the other trail just peters out and you will have to bushwhack down to the creek anyway. The trail is very rocky at this point, and at times it is unclear exactly which is the creekbed and which is the trail. In summer the trail was dry, although after a heavy rain or during the wet season you may find yourself stepping from one stone to another trying to keep dry feet.

The descent is steep at times, especially at the top. After a while the trail turns into an old woods road with rhododendron thickets to the right, where the creek now has its bed for a while.

Shortly after you step across a creek, you will come across a faint trail or woods road to the left. Keep on the main trail, heading downhill. There is another stream to step across amongst rhododendron. The year we were there the rhododendron had only a few blossoms in early July, but in other years they may have more and look spectacular.

You will come quickly to a small clearing with waist-high weeds, back on the old railroad grade. If you turn left here you can walk out along it to Route 635.

The George's Cut Hollow Trail passes diagonally across the railroad grade and continues its downward course through the woods on the other side. Follow it until it gently turns right and runs almost level along the hillside. You will first have to hop over one stream, then pass a muddy spot in the trail. When you come to another stream in a rhododendron thicket, you will be back at the trail junction with the Harvey Hollow Trail a few meters later. Follow the old woods road out, making sure you don't miss the turnoff to Route 635 and your car.

9
Peters Mountain Wilderness

The Peters Mountain Wilderness is a long, rather narrow corridor of 20.2 square kilometers (5,000 acres) on the southeastern flank of Peters Mountain, bordering Monroe County, West Virginia.

Botanically, Peters Mountain is closely related to the Mountain Lake Wilderness, containing much of the same vegetation. The Canadian Zone is represented by hemlocks near the top of Pine Swamp Branch and in some of the other drainages. Additional trees on Peters Mountain include chestnut oak, pitch pine, and upland oaks, mixed with stands of Virginia pine. Throughout the region there are table-mountain pine, yellow poplar, hickory, and red and white oaks. Rhododendron form dense stands in well-watered places, and mountain laurel is plentiful on the higher dry ridges and slopes.

Trout abound in Stony Creek, which, along with County Road 635, forms the southeastern boundary of the wilderness. The rocks are mostly sedimentary, but we did not find any good places to look for fossils.

Average July temperatures in nearby Blacksburg and in Union, West Virginia, are in the low twenties Celsius (seventies, Fahrenheit), but individual days vary greatly. The average January temperatures in these two towns are around freezing, but a record low of minus 37 degrees Celsius (minus 34 degrees Fahrenheit) has been recorded in Union. So, if you are planning a winter camping trip to Peters Mountain, go prepared for very cold weather! And, in any season, take rain gear, for showers are frequent.

In this area we have described the Appalachian Trail in two separate sections—one going southwest and the other northeast from the same spot. The reason for this division is that the second

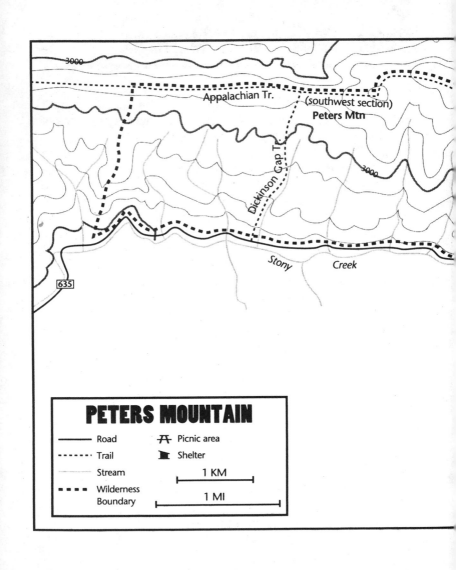

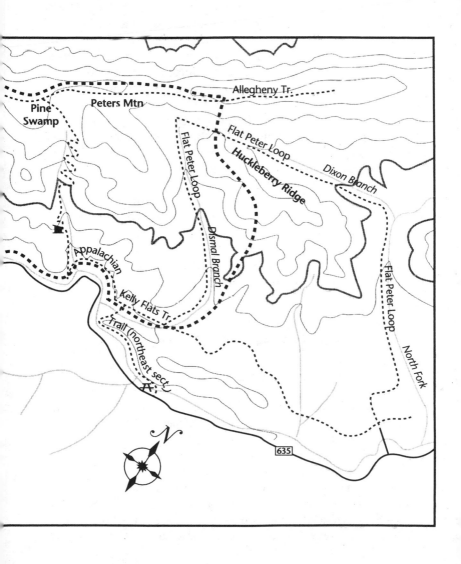

section makes an easy afternoon walk, especially for families with small children. It is about 2.6 kilometers (1.6 miles) long. Only half of that lies within the Peters Mountain Wilderness, but the entire hike is interesting—pretty woods, picturesque streams and hollows, and remains of old mines to explore. If you wish to hike the entire length of the AT within the area, merely join the two sections together. (You will have to read one trail description backward.)

Because the upper reaches of the Dismal Branch section of the Flat Peter Loop Trail are badly eroded, the Forest Service is thinking about rerouting this section of the trail along Huckleberry Ridge, on the edge of the wilderness. No decisions have been made as of this writing.

The Virginia Tech Outing Club has put together descriptions and maps for additional trails not covered here. For information write to Trail Guides, Virginia Tech Outing Club, Box 538, Blacksburg, VA 24060.

No camping or fire permits are presently needed.

Maps: USGS Interior and Lindside quadrangles, 7.5 minute series.

DICKINSON GAP TRAIL

Length: 2.1 kilometers (1.3 miles)
Direction of travel: North
Difficulty: Moderate
Elevation: 640–1,007 meters (2,098–3,300 feet)
Difference in elevation: 367 meters (1,202 feet)
Markings: Blue blazes
Trail #: None
How to get there: Go west on U.S. 460 from Blacksburg, through Newport and Pembroke. Before you get to the first bridge over the New River, turn north on County Road 635. A dirt road with a gate leads off to the left 12.1 km (7.5 mi.) from U.S. 460 (4.5 km or 2.8

mi. past the APG Lime Corporation plant). This is the trailhead for the Dickinson Gap Trail. A double blue blaze is located directly across the road from the trailhead.

You can reach the other end of the trail via the Appalachian Trail (southwest section).

Trail description: A berm blocks vehicular access to the trail, which follows old logging roads all the way to the top of the mountain.

The trail is fairly steep, ascending approximately 1 m in every 6. In places it is very overgrown and blocked by large fallen trees, but it is not really difficult to follow except at the very top, where, if the trail is lost, one need only bushwhack to the AT on the ridgetop. The trail turns several times as it passes through the young-to-maturing forest. At one point it crosses a small stream, which you can easily step over.

At 2.1 km (1.3 mi.) the trail reaches its junction with the AT on top of the Peters Mountain ridge in Dickinson Gap. The Dickinson Gap Trail here is extremely obscure, but the junction is just at the point where a large vertical rock has been painted bright red by surveyors to mark a corner of the wilderness area.

APPALACHIAN TRAIL (SOUTHWEST SECTION)

Length: 27.5 kilometers (17.1 miles)
Direction of travel: Northwest and southwest
Difficulty: Strenuous
Elevation: 719–1,206 meters (2,359–3,956 feet)
Difference in elevation: 487 meters (1,597 feet)
Markings: White blazes
Trail #: 1
How to get there: Go west from Blacksburg on U.S. 460, through Newport and Pembroke. Before you get to the first bridge over the New River, turn north on County Road 635. A sign will point you

toward the APG Lime plant. About 8.8 km (5.5 mi.) past the lime plant (about 16.1 km or 10 mi. from U.S. 460), you will pass a small store. From there drive 0.3 km (0.2 mi.) farther, and park at one of the widened road sections. There is room for one or two cars on the shoulder. A Forest Service sign marks the wilderness area. The Appalachian Trail comes within 20 m of the road, and you can join it via a dirt road on the left just before County Road 635 crosses Stony Creek.

If you wish to hike the trail in the opposite direction, follow U.S. 460 west past the second bridge over the New River. Turn right onto County Road 641 1.1 km (0.7 mi.) beyond the bridge and just before a Subaru dealership. The trailhead for the AT is 0.4 km (0.2 mi.) from U.S. 460. Park on the roadside near the dealership. If you reach a fork on 641, you have missed the trailhead.

Trail description: Enter the woods to join the AT, with its white blazes, and turn left (uphill). After a short steep stretch, the trail slopes gently. In 0.8 km (0.5 mi.) you will arrive at the Pine Swamp Branch Shelter. A nice stream, Pine Swamp Branch, flows nearby.

The trail soon steepens and, after a couple of switchbacks, runs beside Pine Swamp Branch and eventually crosses it. A dense growth of rhododendron shades the stream in this region.

After crossing the stream, the trail ascends the steep hillside via a long series of switchbacks—we counted fifteen—then passes through an attractive, level stretch, the Pine Swamp, where the only conifers are hemlocks. Next the trail ascends again to its junction with the Allegheny Trail on the right. (We have not covered the Allegheny Trail because most of it lies outside the area described here. Signs at the junction show the distance to Waiteville Road to be 20.4 km [12.7 mi.]. From this point to its end at the Mason–Dixon line, the Allegheny Trail runs for 563 km [350 mi.] through West Virginia.) Turn left to follow the AT.

From this point on to the southwest, the AT follows along the ridge of Peters Mountain, which runs all the way to the New River. It stays on the ridge for about 21 km (13 mi.), providing occasional glimpses into the valley on the West Virginia side. The ridge is the dividing line between Virginia and West Virginia and marks the boundary of the Peters Mountain Wilderness.

Long sections of the trail run through thick undergrowth. Where the trail descends rather steeply to Dickinson Gap, occasional large, flat-topped boulders line the ridge.

The very obscure junction with the Dickinson Gap Trail occurs at 7.6 km (4.7 mi.) on the left. Down it, it is 2.1 km (1.3 mi.) to County Road 635.

The AT crosses the southern boundary of the wilderness area 2.1 km (1.3 mi.) past the junction with the Dickinson Gap Trail.

At Symm's Gap, 3.7 km (2.3 mi.) after the Dickinson Gap Trail, an old woods road crosses the AT leading down the slopes into West Virginia (right) and Virginia (left). You will find a fine view of several ridges and valleys in West Virginia here. Then the trees close in around you, and the view is lost.

The trail continues, with many ups and downs, along the ridge of Peters Mountain. It crosses several power lines until it finally descends the mountainside steeply before reaching U.S. 460 and the New River at 27.5 km (17.1 mi.).

APPALACHIAN TRAIL
(NORTHEAST SECTION)

Length: 3.2 kilometers (2 miles)
Direction of travel: Generally east
Difficulty: Easy
Elevation: 719–793 meters (2,359–2,600 feet)
Difference in elevation: 74 meters (241 feet)
Markings: White blazes
Trail #: 1
How to get there: Drive west from Blacksburg on U.S. 460, through Newport and Pembroke. Before reaching the first bridge over the New River, turn north on County Road 635. A sign will point you toward the APG Lime plant. About 8.8 km (5.5 mi.) past

the APG Lime plant (about 16.1 km or 10 mi. from U.S. 460), you will pass a small store. From there drive 0.3 km (0.2 mi.) farther and park at one of the widened road sections. There is parking for one or two cars on the shoulder of the road. A Forest Service sign marks the wilderness area. The Appalachian Trail comes within 20 m of the road, and you can join it via a dirt road on the left just before 635 crosses Stony Creek.

To hike in the opposite direction, continue 2.5 km (1.5 mi.) beyond the bridge across Stony Creek. The AT crosses County Road 635 shortly after the Forest Service's Interior Picnic Area. A signpost marks the intersection. There is a small parking area close by. A sturdy footbridge leads the AT over Stony Creek at this point.

Only the first half of this walk is in the Peters Mountain Wilderness; the second half runs through other national forest property.

Trail description: Follow the white blazes to the right (north), bypassing the left-hand uphill turnoff to the Pine Swamp Branch Shelter.

For a short distance, the trail stays close to the bank of Stony Creek, then crosses Pine Swamp Branch. There are lots of rhododendron here, and they should look spectacular when in bloom. The AT now turns away from Little Stony Creek and gains a little altitude climbing partway up a hillside, but quickly returns to its course parallel to the creek.

The trail continues along the hillside with a few ups and downs. There are several small tributaries to cross, most of them dry in summer. Around these moist creekbeds you will find rhododendron and hemlocks.

Several trailers and a cinder block hunting lodge are situated on the far side of Stony Creek. They can be glimpsed through the trees.

The AT now runs onto an old railroad or mining-car grade. You may even be able to find some old nuts and bolts lying about. The trail follows the grade and turns left with it in front of a stream,

Dismal Branch, where there are a series of picturesque step falls. To see these falls you have to leave the trail and thread your way to the right for a few feet, to the banks of the stream.

There is an old rock foundation on the stream bank near the falls. It may have formed the base for a mill years ago. Or perhaps it was associated with the abandoned mining operations that left a series of graded mounds and stopes for a distance of about 0.8 km (0.5 mi.) upstream. The mounds and stopes are fairly old, as several good-sized trees are growing around them.

The AT now turns right and crosses a small creek. A short grassy spot is followed by a log and plank bridge across Dismal Branch.

Just past this crossing, the AT joins a woods road, which forms part of the boundary of the Peters Mountain Wilderness. Left (upstream), the woods road is the Kelly Flats Trail and leads to the Flat Peter Loop Trail. The AT follows this road to the right for 0.2 km (0.1 mi.), then sharply angles uphill to the left. Some branches have been left across the woods road to indicate the turn. The road itself runs straight ahead to houses and private land.

The AT continues up the crest of a narrow ridge, which it follows for a short way through some rhododendron. It then cuts downhill on the right side of the ridge toward Stony Creek. The descent leads through a pleasant, mature mixed forest, with hemlocks here and there and lots of rhododendron lower on the slope.

The descent down the ridge is fairly steep and the footing is sometimes made difficult by many small stones that slide and roll as soon as you set your foot down.

After reaching the floodplain of Stony Creek, the AT completes the final short stretch under a cool canopy of pines, hemlocks, and occasional holly trees.

At 3.2 km (2 mi.) the trail crosses Stony Creek on a large wooden footbridge to arrive at County Road 635 and the small parking lot.

KELLY FLATS TRAIL

Length: 3.5 kilometers (2.2 miles)
Direction of travel: East
Difficulty: Easy
Elevation: 744–779 meters (2,440–2,555 feet)
Difference in elevation: 35 meters (115 feet)
Markings: Yellow blazes
Trail: None
How to get there: Take U.S. 460 west through Newport and Pembroke. Go north on County Road 635 for 21.7 km (13.5 mi.) until you come to a gravel road. Turn left here and cross a small bridge. Park your car, but be careful not to block a road on the right leading to private property.

The other end can be reached via the Appalachian Trail (northeast section).

Trail description: The Kelly Flats Trail starts with the *left* branch of the road, which also has a gate. The trail follows the road for 1.1 km (0.7 mi.), then enters a long clearing which is initially about 40 m wide, but in one area becomes much wider. Toward the end of the clearing, at 3.5 km (2.2 mi.), the Flat Peter Loop Trail leads off to the right along the Dismal Branch.

Continuing straight ahead on a spur trail you will soon pass through some big rhododendron and come to a wooden footbridge. The trail here becomes an old woods road. Follow it along the hillside and you will soon come to the junction with the AT. A left turn will take you to the Interior Picnic Area at County Road 635. Turn right and you will eventually ascend toward the Pine Swamp Branch shelter.

As its name implies, the Kelly Flats Trail has little change in elevation. Parts of it have been plowed over and cleared for game. In summer, the sun and heat are intense as one passes through the clearings, but there are several attractive meadows adjacent to the trail, and it provides access to other trails that lead to some more beautiful areas uphill.

FLAT PETER LOOP TRAIL

Length: 12.4 kilometers (7.8 miles)
Direction of travel: North–West–South
Difficulty: Moderate
Elevation: 777–1,067 meters (2,550–3,500 feet)
Difference in elevation: 290 meters (950 feet)
Markings: Yellow blazes
Trail #: None
How to get there: Take U.S. 460 west through Newport and Pembroke. Go north on County Road 635 for 21.7 km (13.5 mi.) until you come to a gravel road. Turn left here and cross a small bridge. Park your car, but be careful not to block a road on the right leading to private property.
Trail description: This trail ascends via the North Fork and Dixon Branch to Huckleberry Ridge, then descends via Dismal Branch to the Kelly Flats Trail, which may be followed back to the starting point to form a loop.

Follow the *center* branch of the gated road for 0.6 km (0.4 mi.). The Flat Peter Loop Trail turns right into the woods here. The turnoff is marked with a cairn.

At first the trail follows a property boundary closely along barbed wire. Soon you will see the first of the big rhododendron abundant along this trail. The barbed wire fence veers off to the right, and the trail now follows the North Fork. The forest scenery becomes very beautiful farther along the way.

Shortly after a small cascade, the trail ascends very steeply and there are some wooden steps in the hillside. The trail rises to some vertical rocks, squeezes by, and immediately begins an equally steep descent back down to the North Fork. Here it follows the stream through big rhododendron.

At approximately 1.6 km (1 mi.) there is a footbridge (a flattened log) across the stream. If you don't like it, you can probably hop across the creek on stones.

Continue on the other side of the stream through rhododendron thickets alternating with open woods; the stream is a few feet away to the left. The scenery is lovely, especially when the rhododendron bloom.

The occasional rivulets across the trail have log crossings (on the ground) which may be wobbly, so use care to keep dry feet.

At 3.2 km (2 mi.) you will come to a bulldozed road on your right, and a few steps farther along, the trail will bring you to a bulldozed, circular area where a number of logs were cut.

When we hiked the area, we had to turn to the left and hop across the stream on stones. You will also find the remnants of an old railroad, such as train wheels. The Forest Service was planning to build a footbridge across the stream a few feet to the right of the present crossing, and they may have done so by the time you get there.

Here you leave the North Fork and begin to follow the Dixon Branch. The trail climbs steeply up this valley, meandering back and forth across the stream innumerable times. Watch the trail and the markings carefully. The view of the trail and of the markers is sometimes obscured by fallen timber.

There are also more wet spots in the trail, some of which you can cross on logs.

In summer we heard and saw quite a few black-throated blue warblers in this area. This is a beautiful quiet valley with cool rhododendron thickets. The scenery is well worth the hike.

After about a dozen or so stream crossings, the last of which are mere trickles, you will come to woods with many ferns, which totally overgrow the trail in some places. Watch the blazes carefully—it is very easy to lose the trail here!

Soon you will cross over Huckleberry Ridge and head downhill along Dismal Branch. The ferns do not grow nearly as thickly on the other side of the ridge. Some mountain laurel and rhododendron grow here.

The boundary of the wilderness area runs partly along Huckleberry Ridge and your hike along the Dismal Branch down to the Kelly Flats Trail will be in the wilderness.

Shortly after starting down the Dismal Branch you will come to a stream crossing with lots of fallen trees. The trail occasionally widens to an old woods road, then narrows again. The stream may run over parts of the trail at certain times of the year and after heavy rains.

As you descend the trail you will see more rhododendron thickets, and the trail will become prettier.

At 9 km (5.6 mi.) you will come to the junction with the Kelly Flats Trail. Turn left to return to your starting point, turn right for the junction with the AT.

10
Mount Rogers
National Recreation Area

Mount Rogers National Recreation Area lies in southwestern Virginia near its border with Tennessee and North Carolina, immediately south of the town of Marion. Mount Rogers (1,747 meters; 5,729 feet), Whitetop Mountain to the west (1,690 meters; 5,540 feet), and Pine Mountain to the east (1,685 meters; 5,526 feet) form a ridge of the highest mountains in the state. The northwestern part is the Lewis Fork Wilderness, to the east is Little Wilson Creek Wilderness, and Grayson Highlands State Park lies just to the south.

There are some private inholdings in the recreation area, especially to the south, but no trails cross private property. The one road that does—not described here—is used mainly by people whose livestock graze by lease on national forest land. Grazing, of course, keeps a meadow a meadow.

The area is unique in several aspects. Frazer fir and red spruce grow on the summits of Mount Rogers and Whitetop Mountain. These species are usually found farther south on the higher mountains of the southern Appalachians. At a lower elevation, you will find northern hardwoods such as eastern hemlock, yellow birch, beech, and northern red oak—trees that generally grow much farther north. Below these two distinct zones grow trees much more common to central and western Virginia, such as oak and hickory.

Pine Mountain is a high plateau of open meadows and scattered woods, which give the region an Alpine look. Rhododendron, azaleas, and rock outcrops, as well as grazing sheep, add to that appearance. In the spring you will find many wildflowers in the woods and meadows.

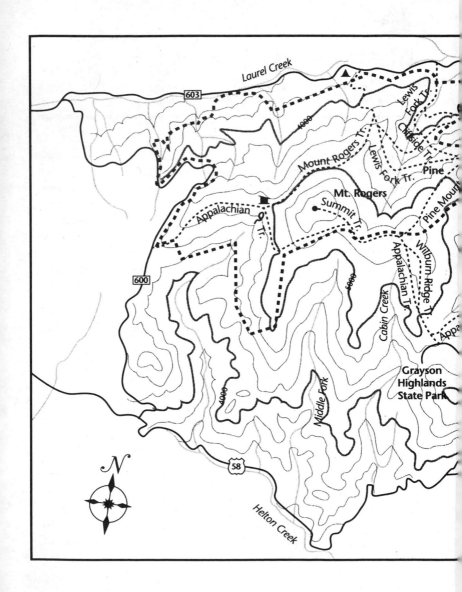

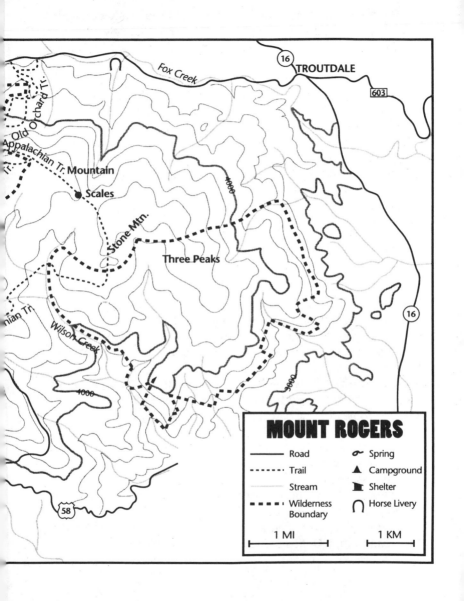

The streams support some fish. Deer and various other animals, as well as a large number of birds, can be observed readily.

If you plan to hike in the recreation area, get a good road map of Virginia. The approach to the region is quite complicated, and you will need the map badly.

About half of the year you can expect frost at night. The mountaintops and high plateaus are snow covered in winter. Summer days are warm, but nights can get chilly. It is not unusual at the higher elevations to have freezing temperatures and snow in mid-May, so take warm clothes.

There are two shelters in the area: Old Orchard on the north slope of Pine Mountain and the other on the East side of Mount Rogers (Thomas Knob). Both are heavily used. Livestock graze in much of the region, especially around Pine Mountain, and the fences you will find across trails are there to confine grazing animals. Unlatch the gates and pass through, but be sure to latch them shut after you.

If you are interested in horses, you may want to stop at the horse livery on County Road 603. Horses can be rented there for a ride along the specially designated trails that have orange markers. Be careful, though, and check your route with the people in the store—certain trails are too rough for horses, and some have suffered broken legs.

A great many horse trails have sprung up in the area. Other trails have been abandoned and receive no maintenance. You can still find some of these paths. Avoid getting lost by carrying a compass and a map.

Many trails have springs running across them and are wet and boggy—often because they have been used by wild ponies as well as hikers. Make sure you wear appropriate footgear.

Maps: USGS Whitetop Mountain and Troutdale quadrangles, 7.5 minute series; High Country Trails, Mount Rogers National Recreation Area, compiled and edited by Larry Landrum, (write Larry Landrum, P.O. Box 247, Blacksburg, VA 24060).

MOUNT ROGERS TRAIL

Length: 7.2 kilometers (4.5 miles)
Direction of travel: South
Difficulty: Moderate
Elevation: 1,098–1,495 meters (3,600–4,900 feet)
Difference in elevation: 397 meters (1,300 feet)
Markings: Light blue blazes
Trail #: 166

How to get there: Use your Virginia road map to get to Troutdale. Then take County Road 603 west for 10.2 km (6.3 mi.) to a small parking area on the side of the road. The trail starts there, on the left (south) side of the road. You can also join the trail via a spur leaving from Grindstone Campground 0.3 km (0.2 mi.) farther along 603.

You can reach the other end of the trail via the Appalachian Trail.

Trail description: Starting on a wooden walkway, the Mount Rogers Trail climbs steadily to its junction with the Grindstone Campground spur at 0.3 km (0.2 mi.).

There are a couple of switchbacks not too far from the campground. After that the trail ascends fairly straight up along the hillside. The first half of the trail is smooth, with few rocks. It climbs through a diverse deciduous forest, comprising magnolia, oak, birch, and beech.

A creek runs for the most part close to the trail, in a little valley of its own. At 3.2 km (2 mi.) the Lewis Fork Trail (dark blue blazes) branches off to the left. After this junction the trail becomes more primitive—rockier and at times also wetter. The forest changes from all hardwoods to a mixture with evergreens. The ferns and mosses under the trees suggest much moisture in the air.

The Mount Rogers Trail traverses the Lewis Fork Wilderness, as does indeed the Lewis Fork Trail, for almost its entire length.

The trail continues to climb on a moderate grade along the side of Mount Rogers until it meets the AT about 7.2 km (4.5 mi.) from the campground. To the right on the AT it is 3.1 km (1.9 mi.) to County Road 600. The Thomas Knob Shelter is approximately 0.3 km (0.2 mi.) to the right on the AT. A blue-blazed side trail leads to a spring.

APPALACHIAN TRAIL

Length: 27.2 kilometers (16.9 miles)
Direction of travel: East and north
Difficulty: Strenuous
Elevation: 1,357–1,647–1,067 meters (4,450–5,400–3,500 feet)
Difference in elevation: 290–579 meters (950–1,900 feet)
Markings: White blazes
Trail #: 1
How to get there: Use your Virginia road map to get to Troutdale. Then follow County Road 603 west for 17.4 km (10.8 mi.) to County Road 600. Turn left (south) on 600 and drive about 8 km (5 mi.) to the grassy saddle between Whitetop Mountain and Mount Rogers. The Appalachian Trail starts on the east side of the road.

For a hike in the opposite direction, go west from Troutdale on County Road 603 for 4.8 km (3 mi.) to the horse livery. The AT starts about 1.5 km (0.9 mi.) past it, on the left.
Trail description: After passing through the gate at the trailhead on County Road 600, you have the choice of following the marked trail (white blazes) to the left or the obvious woods road, which is also a horse trail (orange blazes), to the right. If you opt for the latter, re-member that horses have the right of way. And watch your step!

Hiking along the AT, watch carefully for the blazes; they are sometimes hard to see. At first the AT passes through a meadow, ascending a knob with a good view. Continue across the meadow and cross a stile. The trail generally follows the ridge of Elk Garden Mountain, though it skirts the top.

After an additional 0.2 km (0.1 mi.) the AT meets the Mount Rogers Trail, coming up from Grindstone Campground and County Road 603.

The AT now ascends a rocky, brambly slope then enters a spruce forest. After a couple of switchbacks—sometimes climbing steeply—the trail levels off. About 1.2 km (0.7 mi.) after the junction with the Mount Rogers Trail, the AT makes a sharp left turn. Watch the blazes. It does not cross the fence or go into the meadow beyond. There are some fine views over the fence and across the meadow.

Continue along the AT through the woods. Here the trees are older, and the forest is therefore more open. Several small streams run through the area.

At 6.1 km (3.8 mi.) the trail to the summit of Mount Rogers branches off to the left.

The AT now passes through open meadows with scattered firs, providing truly scenic hiking. At 6.9 km (4.3 mi.) you will come to the Thomas Knob Shelter.

At 8 km (5 mi.), at Rhododendron Gap, a somewhat confusing intersection occurs. Follow the blazes carefully. The AT makes a sharp right turn, while the Pine Mountain Trail—blazed pale blue—continues straight ahead. The Wilburn Ridge Trail, also with blue blazes, runs generally parallel to the AT, crossing over the rock outcrops. You will pass rhododendron thickets—this spot is called Rhododendron Gap—shortly after the trail junction. The flowering bushes look very pretty in early June.

From Rhododendron Gap the AT skirts to the right of Wilburn Ridge and follows a more gentle descent toward Massie Gap in Grayson Highlands State Park. Water can be found along this section of the trail.

After approximately 2.4 km (1.5 mi.) cross a fence—the Wilburn Ridge Trail rejoins the AT shortly before this point—which is the boundary between national forest land and the state park. Shortly thereafter you will come to a trail, blazed blue, leading to Massie Gap in 0.8 km (0.5 mi.).

Here the AT bears sharply left. Follow the white blazes carefully at all times. The trail ascends gradually, crossing and recrossing the boundary between national forest and state park. Wilson Creek even sports a wooden bridge. A horse trail intersects shortly here-after, eventually leading, to the right, to the state park campground.

The AT now skirts a peak, and for a brief stretch you will find yourself in the Little Wilson Creek Wilderness. Then the AT turns north again, crosses another unmarked trail, and passes out of the wilderness.

If you follow the trail to the right you can visit the Three Peaks—some with good views—and eventually loop back to the AT at Scales.

Continuing along the AT, climb toward the crest of Stone Mountain. There are nice views along this stretch. Descend slightly to Scales, where you will find a small fenced-in area, a sort of cor-ral, which mainly serves to keep cattle out—so that you may camp without a cow in your "front yard."

At 21.1 km (13.1 mi.) you will come to the junction with the Pine Mountain Trail, leading back to Rhododendron Gap. Turn right to follow the AT's white blazes.

The trail now descends steadily, winding back and forth. It is fairly rocky in places, and the grade is sometimes steep. The forest changes from evergreen to deciduous woodlands.

At 24.3 km (15.1 mi.) you will arrive at the Old Orchard Shel-ter. There is water close by. The shelter overlooks a meadow. Mount Rogers can be glimpsed to the left.

Just below the shelter the AT crosses a wide trail, blazed blue. This is the Old Orchard Trail, which leads to the Lewis Fork Trail.

Follow the AT downhill through deciduous woods, crossing the Old Orchard Trail once more before meeting County Road 603 at 27.2 km (16.9 mi.).

SUMMIT TRAIL

Length: 0.8 kilometer (0.5 mile)
Direction of travel: Northwest
Difficulty: Moderate to easy

Elevation: 1,647–1,747 meters (5,400–5,790 feet)
Difference in elevation: 100 meters (329 feet)
Markings: Blue blazes; trail easy to follow
Trail #: 4590
How to get there: Via the Appalachian Trail, 6.1 km (3.8 mi.) from County Road 600 or 10.3 km (6.4 mi.) from County Road 603, near Grindstone Campground. The trailhead is located west of Rhododendron Gap, on Mount Roger's eastern slope.
Trail description: At one time the AT crossed the top of Mount Rogers but has now been relocated, and the summit is reached by a short side trail.

This access trail ascends gradually through a somewhat overgrown meadow. It then enters spruce and fir forest. The vegetation remains the same to the summit.

The peak of Mount Rogers is wooded and affords no views. There were quite a few dead and fallen trees on the northeast slopes of the mountain when we were there. A marker is located at the highest point: 1,747 m (5,729 ft.). This is the highest mountain in Virginia.

You will have to retrace your steps to return to the AT and other trails.

WILBURN RIDGE TRAIL

Length: 1 kilometer (0.6 mile)
Direction of travel: Northwest
Difficulty: Moderate
Elevation: 1,418–1,678 meters (4,650–5,500 feet)
Difference in elevation: 260 meters (850 feet)
Markings: Blue blazes
Trail #: None
How to get there: Use your Virginia road map to get to Troutdale. Then drive south on Virginia Route 16 to Volney. Turn right on U.S. 58 and drive 14.2 km (8.8 mi.) to the turnoff to Grayson High-

lands State Park. Take the road into the park and follow it to the trailhead, near a grassy area with picnic tables. Park on the shoulder of the road. The gate into the park is closed from 10 P.M. to 8 A.M., and camping is not permitted within the fenced-in area except in the campground itself.

The other end of the trail can be reached via the Appalachian Trail.

Trail description: Leaving the road in Grayson Highlands State Park, proceed northward up the first part of Wilburn Ridge, reaching the AT after 0.8 km (0.5 mi.). Follow the AT for a short distance to its intersection with the Wilburn Ridge Trail, which then branches off to the right. The fence marks the boundary between the national forest and the state park.

After a short while you will top out on a rise. Then the trail climbs more gently.

The entire area of Wilburn Ridge and Pine Mountain is very open, and bushwhacking presents no problem. You can strike out cross-country at your whim. Do take a compass and a map if you are planning on a bushwhack.

Scattered woods provide a pleasant interruption from the open meadows. The view is excellent along almost the entire trail.

Continue hiking to the northwest. The Wilburn Ridge Trail crosses a number of rock outcrops. Scattered spruce are on your right. Mount Rogers and, in the distance, Whitetop Mountain are to your left.

At 1 km (0.6 mi.) the trail ends at the intersection with the AT. This junction is located near Rhododendron Gap. It is a beautiful area to visit early in June when the bushes are in full bloom.

PINE MOUNTAIN TRAIL

Length: 3.4 kilometers (2.1 miles)
Direction of travel: Northeast
Difficulty: Easy

Elevation: 1,524–1,646 meters (5,000–5,400 feet)
Difference in elevation: 122 meters (400 feet)
Markings: Pale blue blazes
Trail #: 4595
How to get there: Via the Appalachian Trail.
Trail description: Coming from Massie Gap and Grayson Highlands State Park, follow the AT for 3.2 km (2 mi.) to Rhododendron Gap. Here take a right turn onto Pine Mountain Trail. Last time we were there no trail sign could be located, just the pale blue blazes. An orange-blazed horse trail runs parallel to the Pine Mountain Trail for much of the way.

Shortly after the junction, the Pine Mountain Trail descends into a rocky gully. For the first kilometer or so the trail threads its way through shoulder-high rhododendron—a spectacular sight in June when they bloom. Some taller rhododendron and forest follow before the trail reaches open meadows again.

About halfway, at 1.6 km (1 mi.), the Lewis Fork Trail (dark blue blazes) branches off to the left and down the mountain to its junction with Route 603. At this point the distance to the Old Orchard Shelter via the Pine Mountain and Appalachian trails is 5.3 km (3.3 mi.).

The Pine Mountain Trail continues through open meadows, with rhododendron and occasional patches of hardwoods and evergreens, to its intersection with the AT at Pine Mountain. A sign there proclaims the elevation as 1,525 m (5,000 ft.).

From here it is about 3.2 km (2 mi.) to the Old Orchard Shelter via the AT.

LEWIS FORK TRAIL

Length: 7.4 kilometers (5.3 miles)
Direction of travel: Generally east to west
Difficulty: Moderate
Elevation: 1,098–1,519 meters (3,600–4,980 feet)

Difference in elevation: 421 meters (1,380 feet)
Markings: Dark blue blazes
Trail #: 4533
How to get there: From Troutdale, take County Road 604 west for 7.8 km (4.9 mi.) to the sign for the Lewis Fork Trail. There is a stile and a gate at the trailhead. Or you can reach it via the Appalachian and Old Orchard trails or via the Pine Mountain Trail.

This is both a foot and horse trail, so be prepared to meet riders.
Trail description: Start your hike at the stile and gate at Route 603. At times the trail is heavily used by horses, so beware. A second gate marks the Lewis Fork Wilderness boundary.

You will quickly have to cross Lewis Fork. Continue a moderate ascent along a steep hillside on your right. The creek flows beside the trail here, and you can find some pretty spots. There are a number of rivulets crossing the trail, which at times may also be rocky.

At 1.4 km (0.9 mi.) you will reach the trailhead of the Cliffside Trail. This trail, blazed in raspberry pink, goes right, while the Lewis Fork Trail takes a turn to the left towards the Old Orchard Shelter. The Cliffside Trail is too steep for horses.

You will leave the creek after your turn. The trail is quite level here. It passes through a hemlock grove but at times is still rocky and wet.

At about 2.3 km (1.4 mi.) the Lewis Fork Trail meets the Old Orchard Trail. A short distance ahead is the Old Orchard Shelter and the junction with the AT. The Lewis Fork Trail turns right here.

The trail steadily ascends the mountain. For the next 1.3 km (0.8 mi.) the trail becomes wet and rocky. Watch your footing carefully.

You will now cross a tributary creek to Lewis Fork. Just beyond it is a second junction with the Cliffside Trail (raspberry pink blazes). To the left the Cliffside Trail ascends steeply toward the Pine Mountain Trail; to the right it continues its course downhill to its original junction with the Lewis Fork Trail.

Continue following the dark blue blazes of the Lewis Fork Trail uphill. You will cross Lewis Fork again shortly. Many rhododendron grow along its banks. There is no bridge and you will have to hop across on rocks.

After a short, steeper climb the trail forks. The Lewis Fork Trail turns left here, while the right spur leads to the Mount Rogers trail, another short but steep climb.

Except for two small dips across drainage, the Lewis Fork Trail now ascends steeply up the side of Pine Mountain. The trail is mostly wet, often muddy and rocky. Ignore the gate, fence, and horse sign shortly before the junction with the Cliffside Trail.

At 2.7 km (1.7 mi.) the trail meets the Cliffside Trail for a third time—this is the upper end of the Cliffside Trail.

Continue along the Lewis Fork Trail, climbing steeply until you come to a large wilderness boundary sign and the junction with the Pine Mountain Trail at 8.5 km (5.3 mi.).

CLIFFSIDE TRAIL

Length: 2.3 kilometers (1.4 miles)
Direction of travel: North
Difficulty: Easy to moderate
Elevation: 1,171–1,519 meters (3,840–4,980 feet)
Difference in elevation: 348 meters (1,140 feet)
Markings: Raspberry pink blazes
Trail #: 4533B
How to get there: Via the Lewis Fork Trail.
This trail is too steep for horses and is therefore designated for foot travel only.
Trail description: Starting at the top of Pine Mountain, 0.3 km (0.2 mi.) along the Lewis Fork Trail after its junction with the Pine Mountain Trail, the Cliffside Trail branches off to the right.

You will find a large spring at the beginning of the trail, before you leave the open area and plunge into the woods. There is also a hiker walk-through to keep horses from using the trail.

The descent is very steep and, at times, rocky for the first kilometer (0.6 mi.), until the Cliffside Trail crosses the Lewis Fork Trail. You will find another sign prohibiting horses here.

Now the trail becomes much less steep—compared with the first section it feels almost flat here. A number of rivulets, small and large, cross the trail. You will have to pick your way across these, but they should be no problem. And if you find downed trees, climb over them if possible rather than walking around—this lessens erosion.

At 2.3 km (1.4 mi.) the Cliffside Trail meets the Lewis Fork Trail for a third time and ends here. If you continue to the left and downhill you will get to Route 601, to the right are the Old Orchard Trail, the shelter, and the AT.

OLD ORCHARD TRAIL

Length: 2.5 kilometers (1.5 miles)
Direction of travel: South
Difficulty: Easy
Elevation: 1,083–1,226 meters (3,550–4,020 feet)
Difference in elevation: 143 meters (470 feet)
Markings: None
Trail #: 4533A
How to get there: Use your Virginia road map to get to Troutdale. Go on County Road 603 past the horse livery and the intersection with the Appalachian Trail. The Old Orchard Trail starts approximately 2.7 km (1.7 mi.) past the horse livery.

The opposite end can be reached via the Lewis Fork Trail.
Trail description: The trail starts at a gate at County Road 603. This trail is designated for horse and foot travel, so be prepared to encounter some four-legged trail users.

The first few meters are somewhat wet and soggy. Almost immediately after starting, you will have to cross a stream. Your feet may be a bit damp by the time you have negotiated this section of the trail.

The trail works its way gently uphill. Rhododendron grow here, which make for some beautiful hiking when they are in bloom.

For the most part the trail is dry, except in wet weather when you might find wet spots along the length of it.

After about 1 km (0.6 mi.) you will reach the junction with the AT. To the left is Route 603, to the right it continues uphill past the shelter to the top of the mountain and south.

Shortly after the junction the trail turns right, then continues a few meters straight ahead, then turns sharply left to complete a somewhat extended switchback. At 0.3 km (0.2 mi.) from the junction with the AT, a spur trail goes off to the left. This trail is mainly used by horses.

Continue on the Old Orchard Trail on its gradual ascent toward the shelter. Another 0.3 km (0.2 mi.) and the trail turns right along the hillside.

The trail continues wet at times, but never really soggy. Soon you will reach another junction with the AT and the Old Orchard Shelter. Right is Route 603, and to the left the AT climbs the slopes of Pine Mountain.

Just beyond the shelter, the Old Orchard Trail ends at a junction with the Lewis Fork Trail. Straight ahead along the Lewis Fork Trail is the beginning of the Cliffside Trail and Route 603, to the left the Lewis Fork Trail continues uphill to its eventual junction with the Pine Mountain Trail.

Suggested Readings

Walking Softly in the Wilderness, A Sierra Club Guide to Backpacking by John Hart; published by Sierra Club Books, San Francisco, California.

Appalachian Trail Guide to Central & Southwest Virginia; published by the Appalachian Trail Conference, Harpers Ferry, West Virginia. This book contains much useful information on camping and backpacking.

Birds of North America: A Guide to Field Identification by Chandler S. Robbins, Bertel Bruun, and Herbert S. Zim; published by Golden Press, New York, New York. A handy guide for field identification of birds both at home and on the trail.

Trees of North America by C. Frank Brockman; published by Golden Press, New York, New York. A guide to the identification of trees.

About the Author

Karin Wuertz-Schaefer is a member of the Sierra Club and worked for several years on the club's New York staff. She now lives in the Washington D.C. area where she works as a teacher of German, a translator, and a freelance writer.

Karin and her husband, Bob, a physicist, have been involved in local efforts to establish wilderness areas in Virginia. The idea for *Hiking Virginia's National Forests* grew from this involvement. With the help of friends involved in conservation movements, Karin has continued to update and expand the book, now in its fourth popular edition.

Also of Interest from The Globe Pequot Press

Hiking Great Smoky Mountains, Third Ed. $9.95
     Eighty exhilarating hikes in the Smokies

Hiking Rocky Mountain National Parks, Eighth Ed. $12.95
     Most popular guide to this beautiful park

Hiking South Carolina Trails, Third Ed. $12.95
     More than 200 scenic and historic trails

Tennessee Trails, Third Ed. $9.95
     More than 100 of the best hiking and backpacking trails

Canoeing the Jersey Pine Barrens, Fourth Ed. $11.95
     Navigate the waters of this intriguing area

Short Nature Walks on Cape Cod and the Vineyard, Fourth Ed. $8.95
     Twenty-six quiet, beautiful walks in a natural paradise

Short Nature Walks on Long Island, Fourth Ed. $9.95
     Fifty-two walks in wildlife refuges, arboretums, and more

Sixty Selected Short Nature Walks in Connecticut, Third Ed. $8.95
     Sixty walks showcasing the natural beauty of Connecticut

Available from your bookstore or directly from the publisher. For a free catalogue or to place an order, call toll free 24 hours a day 1-800-243-0495 (in Connecticut, call 1-800-962-0973) or write to The Globe Pequot Press, P.O. Box 833, Old Saybrook, Connecticut 06475-0833.